HOT THAI RECIPES

HOT THAI RECIPES

NOI DOK MALEE

foulsham
LONDON • NEW YORK • TORONTO • SYDNEY

foulsham

The Publishing House
Bennetts Close, Cippenham
Berkshire SL1 5AP, England

ISBN 0-572-02188-7

This edition copyright 1997 W. Foulsham & Co. Ltd.
Originally published by Falken-Verlag GmbH
Niedernhausen TS, Germany

Typeset in Great Britain by Typesetting Solutions, Slough, Berks.
Printed by St. Edmundsbury Press, Bury St. Edmunds, Suffolk.

Contents

Notes on the Recipes

- Ingredients are given in metric, imperial and American measures. Use only one set in a recipe, do not try and combine them.

- Always wash and dry fresh ingredients before use and peel where appropriate.

- Preparation times given at the beginning of the recipes are approximate and include the cooking time where necessary. They do not allow for marinating or chilling time.

- All herbs called for are fresh unless otherwise stated. If you are substituting dried, use half the quantity as they are much more pungent.

- In recipes where stock is called for, use fresh where possible (see pages 26 and 27) but bought ready-made stock is a good alternative or you can use stock cubes if necessary.

- Where specialised ingredients are called for a reference to the glossary or an alternative are often given. If in doubt check the glossary at the front of the book for further information.

Foreword

U p until a few years ago Thai cooking was virtually unknown in this country, whereas Chinese cooking has been cooked around the world for a very long time.

Since travelling long distances has become more common and affordable, Thailand too has attracted the attention of tourists interested in cooking and amateur cooks who like travelling.

Thai cooking has been influenced by the geographical position of the land, its historical development, its culture, not to mention its religion – Buddhism. Unlike Chinese cooking, regional differences are hardly noticeable, except that in the north milk (pudding) rice is preferred, whereas everywhere else long-grain rice is most widely used. You will also find that the curries in the south tend to be hotter than elsewhere, but they're often toned down with coconut milk.

It's important in Thai cooking to keep – though not always very strictly – to the recipe directions! In Thailand recipes are passed on orally from generation to generation and so vary from family to family. But the dishes (almost) always remain hot. As our taste buds are not so tough, the number of chillies has been considerably reduced, anyone liking it a little hotter, can certainly add to them and, likewise, reduce the quantity if you're faint-hearted!

Give your imagination free rein, combine the spices as you think – just as a Thai housewife or a Thai cook in a restaurant would do.

As there is little problem these days in obtaining all spices and almost all the different types of vegetables and fruit needed in Thai cooking, it is fairly simple to cook traditional dishes. But in some cases I have given European alternatives to the more unusual ingredients. The results won't be quite so authentic, but they'll still taste wonderful.

Thailand and its Cooking

The roots of the present-day Thais lie in the south of China. A people regarded as barbarians by the Chinese lived in the 6th century BC in the area of Yunnan. They founded the kingdom of Nan Chao. When Kublai Khan and his Mongolians invaded in the 13th century they migrated and settled in what is now Burma, Laos, Cambodia, Vietnam and Thailand. They took over the highly developed culture of the Mon, Lawa and Khmer, the principles of administering a state, carrying on wars, the culture of these people and their religion. In this way the leaders of the Thai slowly increased their power and could soon erect principalities in most provinces. Towards the end of the 13th century an alliance was made between three Thai princes which laid the foundation of the Thai kingdom.

Geography and Climate

Thailand covers an area of about 512,000 sq km and has around 55 million inhabitants. The outline of the mainland looks like an elephant's head, whose 'trunk' reaches to the southern peninsula bordering on Malaysia. In the north, Thailand touches Burma and Laos, in the east Laos and Cambodia, in the west Burma. The southern peninsula is surrounded on the west by the Indian Ocean and on the eastern side by the Gulf of Siam (or Gulf of Thailand).

In the centre of Thailand is the 30,000 sq km plain of the Chao Phraya river – the 'rice bowl' of the country. It is bordered on the north and in the west by hills and mountains. In the north-east stretches the dry plateau of the 'Korat', where very little grows. On the other hand, the southern peninsula supports rich tropical vegetation.

The whole of Thailand is influenced by monsoon winds. There are three seasons: a somewhat moderate, dry period from October to March, then a very hot time from March up to June, and finally the rainy season from June to October. Then the rivers often burst their banks which has one benefit: it leaves mud over all the fields, which nourishes the rice crop.

It is not just rice that grows in Thailand in abundance. The endlessly long beaches of the south are edged with coconut palms, in the tropical forests thrive oranges, lemons and limes, bananas, mangoes, guavas, papayas, lychees and pineapples (at times even growing wild), and a multiplicity of other exotic fruit like durian, jackfruit, rambutan and baelfruit. There are also 'imported' fruit and vegetables, not natural to the area, such as apples, pears, strawberries, grapes and potatoes as well as coffee – they all thrive in Thailand. Also important is the cultivation of maize, sugar cane, soya beans, manioc (tapioca), and tobacco as well as growing bamboo fields, that provides products with many different uses (see also Fruit and Vegetables p.15).

Rice – The Staple Food

R ice is the most important and oldest food in Thailand. The Thai word for eating is the same as that for rice – so its role as the staple food is abundantly clear. Very probably rice originated in Thailand. It was thought for a long time that China was its home until some time ago grains of rice from the period around 3500 BC were discovered in the north-east, that is 700 years earlier than the earliest Chinese finds.

In the heart of the Capital, Bangkok, right next to the king's palace, there is a large field that once served as a market place, but is used today for sporting events and religious ceremonies. Every year in the spring in the presence of the king a portion of the field is ploughed up with two white oxen as a symbolic plea for a good harvest.

For breakfast Thais like to have a bowl of light rice soup and a small bite of fish, meat or vegetables. During the day they will make do with a snack. Thai meals are usually eaten in the evening when white rice stands in the centre of the table. There is no cold starter first, such as we eat, or a soup, followed by the main dish and last of all the dessert, but everything is put on the table at once. Depending on the occasion and the money available, that can be up to nine dishes, which would include a steamed dish, a soup, a fried dish, a curry, a salad or an accompaniment and a sauce or a dip. In addition there would be fresh fruit and on special occasions, one or two sweets.

International Influences

Thai cooking has been influenced most by the Chinese. Many Chinese dishes are still found these days almost unchanged on Thai menus. Chinese cooks, even as far back as the 3rd century BC, considered it very important to offer the five different types of taste at each meal, and these are bitter, spicy hot, sweet, salty and sour. This custom has been taken over by the Thais. This applies also to the Chinese preference of serving different dishes prepared in many ways at the same time, for example a crispy food with a soft one, a fried dish with a boiled, a braised with a steamed, a cold with a hot.

In Thailand chopsticks are not used to eat with, but a fork and spoon. The food is usually served in bite–sized pieces, which goes back to the Chinese habit. Even Confucius would tolerate no knife (even no fork) at the table, as he considered this to be a barbaric killing tool and, he also regarded the sharpening of knives especially at the table, as a great faux pas. He advised noblemen not to visit slaughter houses and kitchens. Even to this day, Buddhist Thais leave the killing of animals, for religious reasons, to Moslems and Chinese living in the country. Nevertheless, eating meat is something they enjoy enormously.

Cutting up food in to mouthful-sized pieces has other reasons as well, all going back through centuries of old Chinese traditions: in this way ingredients requiring different cooking times can be combined and so the possibility for variety is increased.

As a result of this method of cutting up, small left-overs can be used in a variety of ways to furnish other dishes and use up food in a better way. This can be both economical and time-saving.

The Indian influence on Thai cooking is also evident. The preference for highly spiced dishes and the technique of first making a spicy paste and then frying this in a pan together with other ingredients is something Thais have in common with Indians. In India and Indonesia as well as Thailand, the fieriness is reduced using coconut milk.

But there is another thing that connects Thai and Indian cooking: curry. When speaking of curry in Thailand as well as India one does not think of the spice, but a dish prepared with sauce, whether with fish, meat or vegetables. There are two versions of the origin of the word, one is that it comes from the Tamil word kari, which means sauce; the other is that it is a word from the Indian pan kahari, a kind of wok. The English then made from this the word curry thus giving the word quite a different meaning. Today it has come to mean a standard combination of spices made from up to 20 different ingredients. This powder should not be used in the preparation of Asian dishes, but do what Thai and Indian cooks always do and prepare the spice paste fresh yourself.

A curry then, is nothing other than a particular way of preparing a food. First, the spice paste is roasted in a frying pan, the remaining ingredients are added to it along with water, stock or coconut milk. It is then simmered until tender. In Thailand a curry is called gaeng (pronounced ge-eng) and means a full soup or hot pot.

Finally, the Europeans have also influenced Thai cooking and especially the Portugese, known for trading in vegetables, fruit and spices. They brought to Asia, for example, tomatoes and potatoes from South America. But nothing became as popular as the chillies they introduced from Mexico!

Presentation

A Thai meal offers more than just something that tastes good, it ensures that the eye has a feast too. At an official or celebration dinner it will be clear with what imagination and love of detail the Thais cut decorations from vegetables and fruit to make their dishes a real work of art. From carrots, cucumbers or radishes, magnificent blossoms and leaf motifs are created and even whole bouquets! Slices of pumpkin are changed into fish or crabs, melons and pineapples become ships and little baskets that can be filled with food. Banana leaves serve as plates or they are shaped into little bowls in which different food is steamed. An every day meal will, naturally, be less lavishly decorated. For us as Europeans it is certainly difficult to find the necessary patience and to develop the dexterity of fingers of the Thais in order to create such decorations. It is just as effective to decorate the table or serving plates with beautiful exotic flowers or put out shallow bowls of water with the flower heads floating in them.

In some of the recipes I have given instructions for simple garnishes but the really exotic sculptures are best left to the experts!

Seafood

B ecause of its position on the Indian ocean and the Gulf of Siam, Thailand has access to immense riches of fish and seafood. The rivers, too, have an abundance of fish. In order to water the rice fields thousands of kilometres of canals have been built that, just like the flooded rice fields, are all full of fish. In Bangkok the many waterways are called *klongs*. They serve as traffic ways as well as places to live. This is why Bangkok is known as the 'Venice of the East'. These canals too are full of fish.

The most well-loved and finest (but also the most expensive) sea fish is the silver or white pomfret, also pompano. It has a firm, white, and particularly delicate flesh, and is favoured throughout the Indo-pacific area. It is, sadly, not available here but halibut or sole make good alternatives.

Also used in Thai cooking are hake, sea pike (garfish), mackerel, barbel, bream, perch, and tuna fish. Hake, barbel, perch and bream must be scaled before use; if you ask, the fishmonger will do it for you. Fish are often prepared whole, but you can always use fillets instead if you prefer. Thais like large king prawns (jumbo shrimp) very much and they are found for sale in huge quantities in the markets of towns and villages. Besides this, there are prawns (shrimp), crabs, lobster and crayfish, squid, different shellfish, and oysters. Sliced, salted, dried squid is a delicacy. The pieces are nibbled in Thailand like we eat potato crisps (chips).

Equipment and Cooking Methods

Indispensable for making spiced paste is a pestle and mortar. It should be of stone that is not too smooth, to grind spices. Alternatively use a bowl with the end of a rolling pin, or even a coffee grinder (but beware of grinding coffee in it afterwards!). For frying and braising a Thai housewife uses a *khathe* which is roughly like the wok we use here. Naturally, good results can be obtained by using a pan, preferably made of cast iron. If in my recipes I suggest the use of a pan, then use a wok, should you have one. For steaming, bamboo or metal baskets that fit on top of each other are best. These can be placed in a wok or in a deep pan, with some water and closed. Steaming inserts can also be obtained for pots and pans. The Mongolian fire-pot is usually used for keeping soups warm these days.

As a work surface, a sawn off stump of a Tamarind tree is used in many households. At home, it is a good idea to keep a separate chopping board just for garlic and spices.

The most important cooking method is stir-frying. In this way ingredients are cut small and cooked quickly in hot oil, stirred all the time with a spoon or spatula. The whole process lasts only for a few minutes, therefore one needs to be very careful when doing this, that all the ingredients are to hand quite close by. As a result of being stir-fried the ingredients keep their flavour, colour and texture.

When using the stir-fry method, garlic should only be added at the very end as it burns very quickly and can then make the food bitter.

The second most important method of cooking is steaming. In large restaurants and hotel kitchens in Thailand there are huge steam ovens in which there is room for a large number of plates. At home, a steamer is very useful but a large saucepan with a tight fitting lid will do. The ingredients to be steamed are placed on a plate or a flat bowl which is then placed in the saucepan.

The plate should stand up to two thirds in boiling water, and the steam must be able to circulate around the sides. A better method is to place an old saucer or small rack at the bottom of the saucepan and place the dish with the ingredients in it, so that it does not come into contact with the water, but is directly in the steam. If larger pieces of meat are being steamed so requiring a longer cooking time, one must be careful that there is always sufficient boiling water in the pan. Steaming is a particularly protective method of cooking: the foods retain their flavour and minerals and vitamins are not lost in the water. Besides this, steamed foods are low in calories as they can be prepared without fat.

Another method of cooking is braising. For braising a deep pan is best, or a special braising or roasting pan with a lid.

For deep frying, of course, a *friteuse* is ideal. Anyone without one can use a deep pan or a saucepan. For frying the best is a vegetable oil (ground nut (peanut), soya or sunflower oil), but in no case should butter or margarine be used (which are never used in Thai cooking). The fat should be heated to 190°C/375°F or until a cube of day-old bread browns in 30 seconds. The Thai method of testing the temperature is much more novel. A chopstick is dipped quickly into the hot oil, and if it foams up, the desired temperature has been reached. It is best not to fry too many ingredients in one go as the oil will cool off too rapidly and the food will not be able to cook properly.

Grilling (broiling) in Thailand is usually done in the open air on a charcoal grill. The food is often marinated beforehand in a mixture of oil, soy sauce and/or spices. Well-known are the Satay skewers that are widely found in Singapore and Indonesia. Pieces of lean meat are stuck onto bamboo skewers, they are grilled and eaten together with a peanut or coconut sauce.

Drinks

T hais seldom drink alcohol with a meal, instead they drink water, tea or fruit juices. Beer is a good accompaniment to most highly spiced foods, whereas wine is not suitable at all. But if you do wish to drink wine select a dry white wine with a low acidity level.

Basic Foods

R ice is the basic food of Thailand. Around a bowl of steaming rice in a Thai meal will be found the greatest varieties of foods (see page 9).

Do not use any pre-cooked rice, just ordinary white long-grain (Patna) rice, or still better Thai scented rice available in Asian shops or Indian Basmati rice. For 4 people around 350 g/12 oz/1½ cups are required. First the rice is washed under running cold water and rinsed until the water becomes clear. Then the rice is drained and boiled either in plenty of salted water until just tender (about 10-15 minutes), drained and rinsed with boiling water. Or it can be boiled in a good one and a half times its quantity of water in an open saucepan for 5 to 8 minutes on a high heat. Then the saucepan is closed and the rice left to swell on the lowest heat for another 15 to 20 minutes. The rice grains should quite gently stick to each other but not be stodgy.

A third method is to steam it.

Milk rice [pudding rice]
Milk rice is used mostly for sweets. It sticks together in cooking like porridge. In the north and north east of the country it is a main food. Milk rice must be left to swell in cold water for about 2 hours, before actually cooking it in one and a half times its amount of water. It is left to simmer for about 20 minutes.

Fermented rice
It is made from boiled milk rice and sold as a sweet.

Rice flour
Fine flour made from normal long-grain rice. It is used in Thai

cooking as a binding medium and is well-liked for making dough. As a substitute cornflour (cornstarch) or potato flour can be used.

Tapioca flour
Made from manioc (tapioca) a starch-rich root. It is indispensable in Thai cooking and is now available here. It can also be substituted by cornflour (cornstarch) and potato flour.

Rice noodles
They are made from rice flour and sold in different widths, narrow and wide noodles. Mostly the thin rice noodles are used. They are scalded with boiling water, then left to swell for a few minutes then drained. They are then used in dishes as required.

Glass noodles [bean noodles]
Glass noodles are made from mung bean flour and must also be soaked before being further prepared. They are very fine and when cooked become quite transparent.

Egg noodles
These are made from white flour and (duck) eggs and are spaghetti thin. They can be bought under the name *Mie Hoen*. Egg noodles are cooked very quickly in boiling, salted water.

Fruit and Vegetables

Pineapples are frequently used for sweet-and-sour dishes. The fresh fruit must first be carefully peeled, and all the tiny brown 'eyes' must be removed. First the top is cut off along with the bottom end, then it is placed horizontally on a board and the peel slowly cut off from top to bottom with a sharp knife. Then the pineapple is quartered and the core cut out. Finally, the fruit flesh can be cut into pieces.

Unsweetened canned fruit may be used instead.

Aubergines (eggplants)
In Thailand many different varieties of aubergine are known: from the pea-sized green *makeur* through the ping-pong ball-sized white and yellow fruit to the large violet aubergines that we all know. The small makeur are left whole or cut in half, and added to the food when it is almost ready. They can be obtained in Asian shops or

markets with a good selection of fruit and vegetables.

Bamboo shoots
Bamboo is a plant with a variety of uses. Bamboo canes are used in Asia as scaffolding, furniture and objects in daily use, such as cooking utensils and packing are made from it. Chinese medicine uses bamboo shoots because if its high silicic acid content in order to produce medicines for nervousness and mental illness. It is the young shoots of the bamboo bush that are edible. Here they are available canned or in jars. They should be preserved whole as they are of better quality than the finely chopped. The taste of the bamboo shoot is bland but with a nutty texture.

Bananas
In Thailand over 30 different varieties are found growing. They are eaten raw and prepared as a sweet. Besides this, the large leaves can be used like packing paper, or little baskets can be shaped from cut leaves, in which food such as milk rice can be packed to be cooked (see page 145).

Bitter cucumbers
A light green fruit very much like a cucumber with a furrowed, shrivelled skin, that is now available in specialist shops. Other names for it are *Karella* and *Balsam pears*. In Thailand the leaves and the tender shoots of this plant are also eaten. Its taste, as the name suggests, is bitter.

Tongu mushrooms
Also known as *shiitake* mushrooms. They have a pronounced flavour and are usually obtained dried. On the outside, they are similar to large, dark brown cultivated mushrooms. Before preparation they are soaked for 15 minutes in lukewarm water and the hard stalk is then removed. Using a little of the water in which they have been soaked gives the food a more spicy taste.

Chinese radish
Known here as *Winter radish* it is a white radish with a mild taste that is as well-liked in Asia as are carrots here.

Durian
This fruit originates in Indonesia and the Philippines and is highly prized in Thailand. It is as large as a head, yellow-green and with

soft spikes 1 cm/½ in long. Inside the fruit is white and creamy and is not liked by everyone – it smells very pungent like old cheese! It is something only for real connoisseurs.

Guavas
These are the fruit of the evergreen myrtle. They grow from plum to pear size and have a pleasant sour sweet taste, which is reminiscent of a mixture of pears, figs and quince. The fruit flesh is yellow green and changes colour in cooking to salmon pink. They can be eaten raw or cooked. Guavas make wonderful sorbets.

Jackfruit
It is the fruit of a tree from the mulberry family. This southern Asiatic relative of the African breadfruit tree is to be found everywhere in the tropics. The fruit looks like large beet, they are covered in hard skin with knots. Inside it is soft, juicy and sweet and is similar when fully ripe to a fig. Unripe fruit is often cut up small and dried. The seeds taste like chestnuts and are eaten raw, dried or cooked and also ground for flour.

Kaffir limes
A lime with a green wrinkled skin. It contains very little juice, but has an incomparible aroma. Substitute ordinary limes if unavailable.

Coconuts
Here, unfortunately, we can only buy the ripe, dark brown coconuts. In the countries in which coconut palms grow, the green, unripe fruit is also enjoyed and has up to 1 litre/1¾ pts/4¼ cups of coconut milk in the centre. It is a clear, sweet liquid, with which also mixed drinks are prepared. In Thailand as in all tropical countries, these coconuts are offered for sale at street stands and markets, they are often kept chilled in a showcase, a straw is stuck into it and a delicious refreshment is ready.

For sweets usually the green fruit is used whose white flesh is soft and full of flavour. We are obliged to use the ripe fruit, containing hardly any liquid, but instead has a firm white, pleasant tasting flesh. In order to open it, a hole is drilled in one of the dark three 'eyes' and the coconut water drained out. (It can either be drunk as it is or mixed with ice cubes and white rum). Now knock hard with the back of a large knife until it splits and the inside can be removed. If the coconut is to be grated, then the inner brown skin must be removed, that is otherwise eaten with the flesh. In order to produce coconut milk, the coconut flesh is puréed best in a mixer or food processor. Also desiccated (shredded) can be used, but it produces a relatively weak flavour. Pour boiling water or milk over the coconut (approx. 500 ml/17 fl oz/2¼ cups to 250 g/9 oz/2¼ cups fresh purée or 200 g/7 oz/1¾ cups desiccated (shredded)). This mixture is left to stand for 10 minutes and then strained through a sieve (strainer) lined with muslin (cheesecloth). It is then squeezed well with the aid of the cloth. These coconut flakes can be soaked and pressed out a second time, but the result will then be rather thin and weak. If you leave the first pressing to stand for a while, then the so-called concentrated coconut cream will rise to the top. Coconut milk should be prepared in large quantities, when fresh coconuts are available as it freezes well. To cook the milk it is best to stir the cream in with the milk underneath and measure the quantities given in the recipes.

You can buy coconut milk in cans which is a good and labour-saving alternative!

Block creamed coconut can be bought in supermarkets and in Asian shops where it is also called coconut concentrate and sold under the name *Santen*. This concentrate can be diluted to make coconut milk using water or milk, or can be added in pieces to sauces, to melt and give a rich texture and flavour.

Lychees
Lychees are fruit the size of a marble, whose white to pink coloured sweet fruit flesh is enclosed in a leathery shell. Lychees have a perfumed and unmistakeable flavour and are particularly liked in China. They can be eaten raw or as a compote.

Makeur *see* aubergine

Mangostane
The fruit is about 5 cm/2 in in size and hidden under their thick, firm peel contains a light fruit flesh with edible seeds (pits). It is divided into several segments and tastes delicately tender yet sour and refreshing. Mangostane are nearly always eaten fresh.

Mu-err mushrooms *see* cloud ear mushrooms

Oil
In Thailand groundnut (peanut) and soya oil are usually used for

cooking or frying. In some meals before serving a few drops of aromatic sesame oil are added. For deep frying coconut fat (hardened) is traditionally used which should not be confused with hardened coconut creme 'Santen' (see coconut). But any good-quality vegetable oil is fine.

Pak soi
A variety of cabbage well-liked in Asia with a white stalk and large dark green leaves. It is available here but can be substituted by Swiss Chard or Chinese leaves (stem lettuce).

Palm hearts
The marrow of the palm also known as *Palmito*, has the appearance of thick smooth asparagus, is sticky, and is sold here only in cans.

Papaya
Papayas grow on the trunk of a tree looking like a palm. The long oval pear-shaped fruit reach a weight of 3–6 kg/7–13 lb, but only small ones are sold in shops here, each about 450 g/1 lb. Papayas are green and have a light orange coloured fruit flesh with inedible black seeds (pits) which like the pumpkin are found in the centre of the fruit. The flesh is rich in provitamin A and vitamin C. Ripe fruit taste best with a little lemon juice and sugar, as a juice or purée. Unripe fruit can be prepared like a vegetable. The seeds of the papaya contain papain, a splitting protein enzyme. For this reason the seeds are ground to a powder and sold as a meat tenderizing product.

Rambutan
Rambutan fruit is related to lychees. It is a small tree fruit with a bright red shell covered in soft spikes. The fruit flesh tastes sweet and has a flavour like lychees.

Here rambutans are only occasionally obtainable fresh, but are available in cans.

Long beans
These are well-liked all over Asia. Long beans taste very much like our runner beans, but they can grow as long as 50 cm/20 in. They are available in some greengrocers (especially Asian ones) or use runner beans or French beans.

Shiitake mushrooms *see* **Tongu mushrooms**

Soya bean shoots or soya bean sprouts
What we are here talking about are the shoots of the mung bean. Here these are obtainable fresh and in cans or jars. They can be sprouted at home using mung beans too. The taste tends to be bland, similar to bamboo shoots. They remain crisp even after a long cooking time. They should, however, be added at the end to the dish as then the vitamins remain better preserved.

Water chestnuts
These are obtainable here only in cans. They look really like chestnuts, but botanically are quite different – they are the root ends of a water plant. They have a bland taste but a delicious crisp texture. Usually they are found in dishes that are Chinese in origin. Once having opened a tin of water chestnuts, they should be consumed within a few days and make sure that they are always covered in water. They can be frozen, but tend to lose some of their crispness on thawing.

Chinese cloud ear mushrooms
This black variety of mushroom is available here only dried. The mushrooms need soaking for 1–2 hours and then they should be rinsed well under running water, as they often contain earth. They taste somewhat bland.

Herbs and Spices

Basil *see* **Horapa**

Chillies
Without chillies it is hardly possible to prepare a Thai dish. There are a great number of different varieties, from those about 1 cm/ ½ in long, which at the same time are the hottest, to those over 10 cm/4 in long. When you read the ingredients list in recipes in this book that 3-4 chillies are called for, then it is the medium sized 3-4 cm/1¼–1½ in pods that are meant. In Thailand both dried and fresh chillies are used in cooking. Before use, the seeds must be removed from fresh ones and then cut into rings or long strips, the dried ones are crushed along with the seeds.

Be careful! If you rub them between your fingers, under no circumstances rub your eyes or bring them in any other way in contact with mucous membrane. The fieriness is so strong that it causes immediate swelling and an uncomfortable burning.

Dried chillies are available here under the Italian name *peperoncino* or the Malayan name *Iombok*.

Normally Thai dishes contain so many chillies that they are far too strong for our taste. For this reason in this book the number of chillies is reduced. But do not be fooled, the results are still very fiery!

Cumin *see* **cross caraway**

Galgant
Galgant is also known as *Galanga root, Thai ginger, Alpinia* and *Laos*. The yellow spice root with the pink coloured side shoots belongs to the ginger family and is very well liked in Thailand. Thais swear by its digestive assisting properties and drink a mixture of grated root and lemon juice against stomach ache. Galgant is peeled and finely chopped up. It is an indispensible part of almost all spice pastries. It is available from Asian shops. If unobtainable, I have recommended you use a little ground ginger in the recipes. If you want to add a little yellow colour, add a pinch of turmeric too.

Horapa
The three varieties of horapa used in Thailand (*bai horapa, bai mangluk, bai grapao*), from the same family as our *sweet basil* which can be used instead. Horapa is well-liked in Thai cooking. It is usually sprinkled over the finished meal or used as an accompaniment like a vegetable. Bai mangluk has furrier leaves than bai horapa. Bai grapao is also called *holy basil* and has light red leaves. It is only eaten boiled or fried, eg with frogs' legs. Horapa has a taste similar to basil, but tastes slightly of aniseed.

Ginger
It is the spicy root of the ginger plant that is used, that belongs to the same family as galgant. Ginger is one of the best liked as a spice and healing plant all over Asia. The Thais cut from the young rose-yellow roots artistic decorations such as fishes or flowers, and then preserve them in pink vinegar. Candied ginger can be used as an aroma in drinks. For all dishes fresh ginger is preferable as its flavour is far superior to that of dried or candied ginger. Please make certain when buying ginger that the roots are quite full and the brown skin has a slight shine to it – then they are fresh.

Wrapped up in a damp cloth ginger can be kept in the fridge for some time. It can also be peeled, grated finely, and frozen.

Ground ginger can be used instead, but the flavour is not the same.

Jasmin
These wonderfully scented white blossoms are made into an essence (extract) that is then used to perfume sweets. Be careful, two drops are sufficient of this very strongly scented substance! Jasmine essence can be obtained in all well-stocked Asian shops. Should you not be able to obtain it then use rose water (from the chemists).

Kaempferia
It is the yellow-brown root of the spice lily that is primarily used for fish dishes. Unfortunately, this is not (yet) obtainable here.

Cardamom
Cardamom is not used a great deal in Thailand, except for some curry spice mixtures. It is obtainable whole, that is to say in capsules that need to be broken open before use in order to get at the tiny seeds, that are then ground or crushed. In Thailand the leaves of the plant are also used, but not very often.

Coriander (cilantro)
In Thailand the roots, the leaves and the seed of the coriander plant are used. In this country the root is very difficult to obtain, whereas the seed is well-known as a spice. Thai cooking without the small green leaves is unthinkable and because of its characteristic taste cannot be replaced by parsley except as a garnish if necessary. Usually the leaves are chopped or left whole and sprinkled over a dish just before serving. They are readily available here and freeze well for use chopped.

Cross caraway
We know it as *cumin* but it is also known as *Turkish* or *Asian caraway*. A fragrant spice which has nothing in common with the caraway we know. It is popular in the Near and Far East as well as in the whole of Latin America and it is a key ingredient in Thai cookery.

Curcuma

Better known to us as *turmeric*, this spice is also called yellow spice. It is a root related to ginger and in Thailand is used primarily for colouring. It was used at one time to dye the yellow robes of monks. These days it is an ingredient used in curry powder and for colouring rice dishes. It has a mild, slightly bitter taste.

Pandanus leaves

The leaves of this small sugar palm tree are used to add colour and flavour to desserts, biscuits and drinks. Unfortunately they are very difficult to obtain here. Try using borage leaves instead for flavour. For colour, a few drops of green colouring will do.

Pepper

White and black pepper is used in Thai cooking just as we do, it is an indispensible part of the many spice and chilli pastes.

Tamarind

The fruit of the taramind tree are about 15–20 cm/6–8 in long, flat pods in which the seeds are to be found hidden inside, and are enclosed in a dark brown, sticky mass. The tamarind tree was originally found in Africa, but today is found all over Latin America and South-east Asia. Other names are *Indian dates* and *sour dates*.

To make tamarind juice, soak 25 g/1 oz/2 tbsp fresh or dried pods for up to 20 minutes. Squeeze out as much pulp as possible then strain the liquid through a sieve (strainer). If storing the juice, bring it to the boil, then cool and store in a screw-topped jar in the fridge. Lemon juice can be used instead but it is a poor substitute.

Diluted and sweetened, tamarind juice makes an excellent thirst quencher called *Asem*.

Cinnamon

Cinnamon is used in the preparation of a number of curry pastes and sauces. Use either a piece of cinnamon stick or a suitable amount of ground cinnamon.

Lemon leaves

The leaves of the lemon tree are used, as we use bay leaves in dishes, right at the beginning and cooked with the food. They can be substituted by grated lemon rind or use a whole lemon cut in half which is removed before serving.

Lemon grass
This is one of the very typical ingredients of Thai cooking. The grey-green leaves of this reed-like plant, whether fresh or dried, in pieces or ground, give off a fresh lemon-like flavour and give the food an unmistakeable character. Available in some supermarkets.

Ready-Made Products

Oyster sauce
A sweet-salty tasting, dark brown, thick liquid spice sauce made of oyster extract. It is used to season some dishes during cooking and also afterwards at the table. It is readily available here.

Chilli sauce
A ready-made sauce made of chillies, sugar and vinegar with a piquant sweet-sour taste. It is easily obtainable.

Chinese preserved vegetables
Also known as *Schezuan Pickles* in Asian shops. They are salted vegetables such as gherkins (cornichons), cabbage, radishes and ginger, seasoned with soy sauce. They taste salty-sharp.

Salted beans
These are brown or black beans that are preserved in salt and give food a particular taste. They are available canned in Asian shops and should be rinsed well before use.

Fish sauce
Called *Nam Pla*, it is an important flavouring in Thai cooking. It is clear and brown and is made of a fish and crab concentrate. Mostly it is used to season completed dishes instead of salt.

Alternatively use Anchovy essence (extract) blended with a little garlic and light soy sauce.

As fish sauce does not have a strong taste of fish, it can also be used to season meat dishes and as a simple dip with lemon juice and chillies stirred in.

Prawn (shrimp) paste *(see* Crab paste)

Dried prawns (shrimp)
Small dried prawns (shrimp) with an orange red colour. They are usually used finely chopped. You can use prawn paste instead.

Crab paste
Also known as prawn (shrimp) paste or *Trassi*, it is made from salted, preserved, or dried prawns (shrimp). Available in small blocks from Asian stores.

Palm sugar
This dark brown sticky sugar from the sap of the Palmyra palm is a most popular form of sweetening in Thailand. It is available from Asian shops, but soft brown sugar can be used instead. Palm sugar is not as sweet as normal sugar and tastes slightly of caramel.

Sambal oelek
A sharp Indonesian paste made from red chillies, salt and oil. It is available from Asian shops and specialist grocers. Use sparingly – it is very strong.

Soy sauce
In Thailand there are two types: light and dark sauce. The light soy sauce is light brown and transparent and is used like fish sauce. The dark soy sauce is almost black and opaque and tastes salty-sweet. If it is not possible to obtain Thai soy sauces, then use Chinese, Japanese or Indonesian (*ketjap manis*) ones instead.

Tofu
In Thailand there are many different kinds of Tofu or soya bean curd, and it is available there as salted, unsalted, firm and soft, yellow, white and fermented. The firm tofu is used for fried dishes (sautées) whereas the soft is used as an ingredient for soups and sauces. Fermented tofu is firm, because it has been preserved in a salt solution. You can buy both firm and smooth varieties in super-markets and healthfood shops.

Wan-tan dough sheets
They are usually 10 cm/4 in squares, and are available in Asian shops or in specialist grocers, frozen or vacuum packed. In Chinese they are called *han tan* and literally translated it means 'swallowing a cloud'. Wan-Tans (filled pastry pockets) are served in a soup or as a small snack. They are sometimes filled with meat or fish, sometimes with vegetables (see page 40).

You could substitute filo pastry if necessary.

Chicken Stock

NAM SUP KAI

PREPARATION TIME: 3½ HOURS
MAKES ABOUT 1.5 litres/2½ pts/6 cups

---

1 boiling fowl with giblets

2 onions, roughly chopped

3 garlic cloves, chopped

5 cm/2 in piece root ginger, chopped

2–3 carrots, roughly chopped

1 leek, roughly chopped

3 sticks (ribs) celery, chopped

2.5 litres/4½ pts/11 cups water

Salt

1 Cut the chicken into six to eight pieces, rinse them and place them in a large saucepan.

2 Add the vegetables together with the water and salt to the chicken and bring to the boil.

3 Skim the surface, reduce the heat, half cover with a lid and simmer very gently for 3 hours.

4 Strain and leave to cool. Remove the fat, then use the stock, or freeze in useable portions.

Fish Stock

NAM SUP PLA

PREPARATION TIME: 2 HOURS
MAKES ABOUT 2 litres/3½ pts/8½ cups

---

2 kg/4½ lbs sea fish scraps (head and bones)

2 onions, roughly chopped

4 garlic cloves, chopped

2 carrots, roughly chopped

2 bay leaves

1 lemon, quartered

Salt

10 white peppercorns

3 litres/5¼ pts/12⅔ cups water

1 Place the fish scraps in a large saucepan.

2 Add remaining ingredients.

3 Bring to the boil and skim surface. Reduce heat, half-cover with a lid and simmer gently for 1½ hours.

4 Strain and leave the stock to cool. Use or freeze in useable portions.

Sharp Sauce

NAM PRIK

PREPARATION TIME: 10 MINUTES
MAKES ABOUT 150 ml/¼ pt/⅔ cup

This sauce is served with almost any dish.

8 garlic cloves, crushed

5 dried chillies, crushed

30 ml/2 tbsp dried prawns (shrimp) (or prawn (shrimp) paste see page 25)

5 ml/1 tsp salt

15 ml/1 tbsp sugar

45–60 ml/3–4 tbsp fish sauce (see page 24)

45–60 ml/3–4 tbsp lime or lemon juice

2–4 fresh red chillies, seeded and sliced

1 Purée the garlic with the dried chilli pods, dried prawns, salt, sugar, fish sauce and lime juice in a blender or food processor.

2 Add the sliced chillies to the sauce and stir well.
It will keep for several weeks stored in a screw-topped jar in the fridge.

Sweet Fish Sauce

NAM PLA WAN

PREPARATION TIME: 25 MINUTES

MAKES ABOUT 200 ml/7 fl oz/scant 1 cup

6 shallots or 2 onions,
 finely chopped

8 garlic cloves, crushed

30 ml/2 tbsp oil

3 dried chillies, crushed

75 ml/5 tbsp fish sauce
 (see page 24)

15–30 ml/1–2 tbsp palm or soft
 brown sugar

30 ml/2 tbsp tamarind juice
 (see page 23)

2 spring onions (scallions),
 chopped

30–45 ml/2–3 tbsp chopped
 coriander (cilantro)

1 Fry (sauté) the shallots and garlic in the oil until softened, stirring. Add the chillies and fry until golden brown.

2 Bring the fish sauce to the boil in a small saucepan, add the sugar and tamarind juice and stir until the sugar has dissolved.

3 Add the spring onions and coriander to the sauce then stir in the chilli mixture. Pour into a small dish. Serve at room temperature with almost any meal.

Chilli Ginger Sauce

LON PRIK KHING

PREPARATION TIME: 15 MINUTES
MAKES ABOUT 250 ml/8 fl oz/1 cup

This sauce will keep for a long time in the fridge. It goes well with spring rolls (pp. 42 and 43) and little prawn balls (p.47), and also particularly well with cold meat especially smoked pork and poultry.

---

200 g/7 oz/scant 1 cup sugar

200 ml/7 fl oz/scant 1 cup hot water

2.5 cm/1 in piece root ginger, grated

30 ml/2 tbsp soy sauce

90 ml/6 tbsp red wine vinegar

5 ml/1 tsp salt

5 ml/1 tsp black pepper

5 ml/1 tsp sambal oelek (see page 25)

5 ml/1 tsp cornflour (cornstarch)

1 Caramelise the sugar in a saucepan until light brown. Only stir when the sugar begins to melt at the edges. Then add the hot water, stirring all the time. Be careful, it will splutter so cover your hand.

2 Add the ginger to the saucepan with the soy sauce, vinegar, salt, pepper and Sambal Oelek. Bring to the boil, reduce heat and simmer, for 10 minutes.

3 Blend the cornflour with 30 ml/2 tbsp of water until smooth, add to the boiling sauce and bring once to the boil. Store in the fridge in screw-topped jars.

Chilli Fish Sauce

NAM PRIK PLA

PREPARATION TIME: 20 MINUTES
MAKES ABOUT 300 ml/½ pt/1¼ cups

Serve the sauce with raw or boiled vegetables, for example with cauliflower, okra (ladies fingers), asparagus, white cabbage, green beans and carrots.

5-6 fresh or dried red chillies, seeded and chopped

5 shallots or 1 onion, finely chopped

3 garlic cloves, crushed

225 g/8 oz/½ lb cod or rosefish fillet

150 ml/¼ pt/⅔ cup water

15 ml/1 tbsp prawn (shrimp) paste (see page 25)

5 ml/1 tsp salt

2 spring onions (scallions), chopped

Handful of chopped coriander (cilantro)

1 Pound chillies, shallots and garlic in a pestle and mortar or in a bowl with the end of a rolling pin.

2 Dice the fish fillet and simmer in the water until just cooked. Drain, reserving the water, and flake the fish. mix with the chilli paste. Add enough of the reserved water to make a spooning sauce. Season with prawn paste and salt.

3 Turn into a serving bowl and sprinkle with chopped spring onions and coriander.

Coconut Ham Sauce

LON MAPRAO

PREPARATION TIME: 20 MINUTES
MAKES ABOUT 600 ml/1 pt/2½ cups

Serve the sauce with raw or cooked vegetables like cucumber, cabbage, green beans, carrots and green salad.

500 ml/17 fl oz/2¼ cups
  coconut milk

200 g/7 oz/1¾ cups finely
  diced boiled ham

2 shallots or 1 small onion,
  finely chopped

3–6 fresh red chillies, seeded
  and sliced thinly

100 g/4 oz/1 cup boiled rice

45 ml/3 tbsp tamarind juice
  (see page 23)

15 ml/1 tbsp palm or soft
  brown sugar

5–10 ml/1–2 tsp salt

1 Mix the coconut milk with the ham, rice, shallots and chillies in a saucepan and bring to the boil. Reduce heat and simmer gently, stirring occasionally, for 10 minutes until mixture is a paste-like consistency.

2 Season with tamarind juice, sugar and salt.

3 Use as required.

Coconut Soy Sauce

LON TAO CHIAO

PREPARATION TIME: 40 MINUTES
MAKES ABOUT 375 ml/13 fl oz/1½ cups

4 shallots or 2 onions

25 g/1 oz/¼ cup minced (ground) pork

30 ml/2 tbsp oil

400g/14 oz can salted soya beans

3–5 fresh red chillies, seeded and thinly sliced

25 g/1 oz/2 tbsp peeled prawns (shrimp), chopped

45 ml/3 tbsp sugar

45 ml/3 tbsp tamarind juice (see page 23)

300 ml/½ pt/1¼ cups coconut milk

Salt (optional)

1 Chop half the shallots or onions. Fry (sauté) with the pork in half the oil until meat is browned and onion softened.

2 Purée in a food processor or blender with the contents of can of beans, the chillies, prawns, sugar and tamarind juice.

3 Place in a saucepan with the coconut milk and simmer, stirring occasionally until thick and creamy. Season if necessary.

4 Meanwhile, cut the remaining two shallots into rings, and fry (sauté) in remaining oil until crisp and golden. Drain on kitchen paper.

5 Pour sauce into a serving dish, sprinkle with the shallot rings and serve with raw or boiled vegetables.

Red Spice Paste

KRUNG GAENG PED

PREPARATION TIME: 20 MINUTES
MAKES ABOUT 100 g/4 oz/¼ cup

20 small dried chillies, crushed

6 shallots or 2-3 onions, finely chopped

6 garlic cloves, crushed

15 ml/1 tbsp ground coriander (cilantro)

15 ml/1 tbsp ground cross caraway or cumin

15-30 ml/1-2 tbsp grated root ginger

5-10 ml/1-2 tsp salt

15 ml/1 tbsp black pepper

Grated rind of 1 lime

5 ml/1 tsp grated lemon grass

15 ml/1 tbsp prawn (shrimp) paste (see page 25)

75-90 ml/5-6 tbsp oil

1 Pound all ingredients together to a smooth paste in a pestle and mortar or in a bowl with the end of a rolling pin.

2 Pour into a small screw-topped jar and store in the fridge. The paste can be served with any dish.

Green Spice Paste

KRUNG GAENG WAN

PREPARATION TIME: 20 MINUTES
MAKES ABOUT 175 g/6 oz/¾ cup

6-8 fresh green chillies,
seeded and chopped

2 shallots or 1 onion, finely
chopped

4 garlic cloves, crushed

Handful of coriander (cilantro),
chopped

30 ml/2 tbsp prawn (shrimp)
paste (see page 25)

15 ml/1 tbsp grated root ginger

15 ml/1 tbsp grated kachai root
or chopped mint

15 ml/1 tbsp ground coriander
(cilantro)

15 ml/1 tbsp ground cross
caraway or cumin

15-30 ml/1-2 tbsp black
pepper

2.5ml/½ tsp ground cloves

15 ml/1 tbsp grated nutmeg

15 ml/1 tbsp grated lemon
grass

Grated rind of 1 lime or small
lemon

5 ml/1 tsp salt

90-120 ml/6-8 tbsp oil

1 Pound all the ingredients
together in a pestle and mortar
or in a bowl with the end of a
rolling pin or purée in a food
processor or blender.

2 Pour into a small screw-topped
jar and store in the fridge.
Serve with any dish.

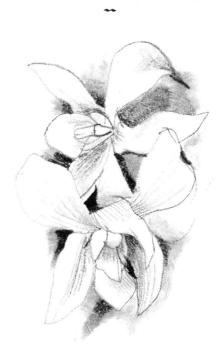

Roasted Chilli Paste

NAM PRIK PAO

PREPARATION TIME: 20 MINUTES
MAKES ABOUT 100 g/4 oz/¼ cup

8–10 dried chillies, crushed

3 shallots or 1 onion, finely chopped

4 garlic cloves, crushed

30 ml/2 tbsp prawn (shrimp) paste (see page 25)

15 ml/1 tbsp sugar

15–30 ml/1–2 tbsp fish sauce (see page 24)

45 ml/3 tbsp oil

1 Pound all the ingredients except the oil to a paste in a pestle and mortar or use a bowl and the end of a rolling pin.

2 Heat the oil in a frying pan (skillet) and fry (sauté) the paste for 2 to 3 minutes over a moderate heat, stirring all the time.

3 Leave to cool then store in a small screw-topped jar in the fridge. It can be served with any dish.

Prawn and Chilli Dip

NAM PRIK KAPI

PREPARATION TIME: 20 MINUTES
SERVES 4

30 ml/2 tbsp prawn (shrimp)
paste (see page 25)

3 garlic cloves, crushed

15 ml/1 tbsp chopped dried
prawns (shrimp) or use extra
prawn (shrimp) paste

2–3 fresh red chillies, seeded
and chopped

3–4 small makeur (see page
15), finely chopped or
30 ml/2 tbsp finely chopped
aubergine (eggplant)

45 ml/3 tbsp lemon juice

45 ml/3 tbsp fish sauce
(see page 24)

15 ml/1 tbsp sugar

1 Dry-fry the prawn paste in a
frying pan (skillet) until it
gives off an aroma.

2 Purée in a blender or food
processor with remaining
ingredients (or use a pestle and
mortar).

3 Serve the dip with raw or
cooked vegetables and with
fried and grilled fish.

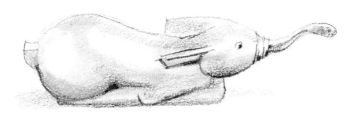

Appetisers and Side Dishes

*Here is a wonderful variety of small
dishes – cold and warm, steamed and
crispy fried, spicy hot and mild.
They may be served to awaken the taste
buds before the main course or a selection
can be served together for a delicate
celebration meal.
They also make perfect accompaniments
to more substantial dishes.*

Filled Pastry Pockets

W A N - T A N

PREPARATION TIME: 1½ HOURS
MAKES 20

FILLING 1:

1 small onion, finely chopped

1 garlic clove, crushed

225g/8 oz/2 cups minced (ground) pork

15 ml/1 tbsp oil

Pinch of white pepper

10 ml/2 tsp fish sauce (see page 24)

7.5 ml/1½ tsp ground coriander (cilantro)

1 egg, beaten

OR FILLING 2:

1 small onion, finely chopped

2–3 garlic cloves, crushed

15 ml/1 tbsp oil

150g/5 oz/ 1¼ cups bean sprouts, chopped

100 g/4 oz/1 cup chopped leeks

15 ml/1 tbsp grated root ginger

10 ml/2 tsp soy sauce

1 egg, beaten

20 wan-tan dough sheets (see page 25)

25 ml/1½ tbsp flour

25 ml/1½ tbsp water

Coconut or other oil for frying

FILLING 1:

1 Fry (sauté) the onion and the garlic with the minced meat until brown. Cool slightly.

2 Stir in the pepper, fish sauce, coriander, and the egg.

OR FILLING 2:

1 Fry (sauté) the onion and the garlic in the oil until golden.

2 Add the bean sprouts, leek and ginger and stir-fry for 3 minutes. Remove from the heat, stir in the soy sauce and egg.

3 Lay the pastry sheets side by side on a damp cloth. Blend the flour with the water and brush the pastry edges with it. Place 15 ml/1 tbsp filling on one half of each sheet, then fold over the other half, pressing the edges together.

4 Heat oil to 190°C/375°F or until a cube of day–old bread browns in 30 seconds. Deep-fry the pastry pockets a few at a time until golden brown. Drain on kitchen paper.

Tapioca Balls Filled with Meat

SAKU SAIMKHU

PREPARATION TIME: 50 MINUTES
PLUS SOAKING TIME
MAKES 20

200 g/7 oz/good 1 cup tapioca
flakes (see Cook's tips below)

75 ml/5 tbsp hot water

1 small onion, finely chopped

30 ml/2 tbsp oil

8 garlic cloves, finely chopped

200 g/7 oz/1¾ cups minced
(ground) pork

40 g/1½ oz/⅓ cup ground nuts

Salt and pepper

5 ml/1 tsp ground coriander
(cilantro)

4 fresh red chillies, seeded
and chopped

COOK'S TIPS: *If you don't have a
steamer, place the tapioca balls in a
greased ovenproof dish. Cover with foil
and stand dish in a deep baking tin
(pan) filled with hot water. Bake in
the oven at 200°C/400°F/gas mark 6
for 30 minutes.*

*Tapioca flakes are made from manioc
roots and are obtainable from specialist
shops. Alternatively, use semolina
(cream of wheat).*

1 Stir the tapioca flakes into the
hot water and leave to swell
for 1 hour.

2 Fry (sauté) the onion in half
the oil until golden. Add half
the garlic, the minced meat,
ground nuts, seasoning, coriander
and half the chillies and stir fry
until crispy brown. Place on one
side.

3 Scoop out little pieces of the
tapioca dough using a small
spoon then flatten into pancakes
about the size of a small plate
using dampened hands.

4 Place a small spoonful of the
filling on each, fold the
pancake and then roll into a ball;
be careful to cover filling
completely.

5 Steam in batches (so they
don't stick together) on lightly
greased foil in a steamer for 15
minutes.

6 Fry the remaining garlic and
chillies in remaining oil until
brown. Drain and sprinkle over the
little tapioca balls.

Spring Rolls with Chicken

HAE KAI

PREPARATION TIME: 1½ HOURS
MAKES 20

FILLING:

1 onion, finely chopped

1 garlic clove, crushed

15 ml/1 tbsp oil

150 g/5 oz/1¼ cups finely chopped or grated carrots

200 g/7 oz/1¾ cups chopped chicken breast

150 g/5 oz/1¼ cups bean sprouts, chopped

5 ml/1 tsp fish sauce (see page 24)

5 ml/1 tsp soy sauce

Pinch of pepper

5 pastry (paste) sheets for spring rolls (or use filo pastry) each 20×20 cm/ 8×8 in, thawed if frozen

1 egg yolk

Coconut or other oil for deep-frying

To serve: Chilli Ginger Sauce (page 30)

1 Fry (sauté) the onion and the garlic in the oil until golden. Add the carrots and the meat and fry for 3 minutes, stirring. Add the remaining filling ingredients and cook for 1 minute, stirring.

2 Cut each of the pastry sheets into four squares and brush the edges with egg yolk. Quickly divide the filling among the squares, fold over on two sides and then roll up.

3 Heat the oil to 190°C/375°F or until a cube of day-old bread browns in 30 seconds. Deep-fry a few at a time until golden brown, about 4 minutes. Drain on kitchen paper. Serve with Chilli Ginger Sauce.

Spring Rolls with King Prawns

HAE KOON

PREPARATION TIME: 1¾ HOURS
MAKES 20

8 dried tongu mushrooms (shiitake)

10 large king prawns (jumbo shrimp) with shells

Salt

2 spring onions (scallions), cut in 1 cm/½ in pieces

1 carrot, chopped

50 canned bamboo shoots, drained and diced

100 g/4 oz/1 cup minced (ground) pork

1 small egg, beaten

15 ml/1 tbsp fish sauce (see page 24)

White pepper

2.5 ml/½ tsp ground coriander (cilantro)

10 square spring roll, wan-tan or filo pastry (paste) sheets, thawed if frozen

1 egg white

Oil for deep-frying

To serve: Chilli Ginger Sauce (see page 30)

1 Soak the mushrooms in luke-warm water for 15 minutes.

2 Break the king prawns out of their shells, leaving the tail fins on. Halve the prawns lengthways and remove the dark vein. Season lightly with salt.

3 Cut off and discard the stalks of the mushrooms and coarsely chop the caps.

4 Mix the prepared vegetables with the minced meat, egg, fish sauce, a little pepper and salt and the coriander. Knead together well with the hands.

5 Spread out the sheets of pastry on a damp cloth and halve diagonally. Brush the edges with egg white. Spread a little of the filling on each halved sheet of pastry, then place half a king prawn on each and roll up the pastry sheet, leaving the prawn tails sticking out.

6 Heat oil for deep-frying to 190°C/375°F or until a cube of day-old bread browns in 30 seconds. Deep-fry the spring rolls for about 4 minutes, turning once. Drain on kitchen paper. Serve with Chilli Ginger Sauce.

Aubergines in Batter

PAD MAKENA YAO

PREPARATION TIME: 1½ HOURS
MAKES 10–15

FILLING:

200 g/7 oz/1¾ cups mixed
   minced (ground) meats

1 egg, beaten

Salt

Black pepper

5 ml/1 tsp soy sauce

5 ml/1 tsp fish sauce
   (see page 24)

5 ml/1 tsp ground coriander
   (cilantro)

5 ml/1 tsp ground cross
   caraway or cumin

1 small aubergine (eggplant)

BATTER:

100 g/4 oz/1 cup plain (all-
   purpose) flour

1 egg

45 ml/3 tbsp oil

120 ml/4 fl oz/½ cup water

Flour for dusting

Oil for deep-frying

To serve: Chilli Ginger Sauce
   (see page 30)

1 Knead together all the filling
   ingredients except the
aubergine.

2 Trim and thinly slice aubergine
   lengthways in 10 or 15 slices.

3 Whisk the batter ingredients
   together with a pinch of salt
until smooth.

4 Spread a little of the filling on
   each aubergine slice, roll up.

5 Dust with flour then dip into
   the batter with a fork, deep-fry
for about 5 minutes until golden
brown. Drain on kitchen paper
and serve with Chilli Ginger
Sauce.

King Prawns with Rice Noodles

PAD MI KUNG

PREPARATION TIME: 40 MINUTES
SERVES 4–8

200 g/7 oz/1¾ cups rice noodles

16 large peeled king prawns (jumbo shrimp)

Salt and pepper

4 egg whites, lightly beaten

Oil for deep-frying

To serve: Chilli Ginger Sauce (see page 30)

COOK'S TIP: Try crab sticks cut in half lengthways in place of prawns for a cheaper alternative.

1 Soak the noodles according to packet directions. Drain and press out all moisture and place in a shallow bowl.

2 Carefully remove the dark vein down the back of each king prawn and season with salt and pepper.

3 First dip the prawns on a fork in the egg white, drain off excess then turn in the rice noodles. Deep-fry in the hot oil for about 2 minutes until crisp and golden.

4 Drain on kitchen paper and serve with Chilli Ginger Sauce.

Filled Egg Nets

R U M E

PREPARATION TIME: 1 HOUR
SERVES 6–8

1 large onion, chopped

6 garlic cloves, crushed

15 ml/1 tbsp oil

450 g/1 lb minced (ground) pork

5 ml/1 tsp salt

5 ml/1 tsp sugar

2.5 ml/½ tsp white pepper

45 ml/3 tbsp soy sauce

5 ml/1 tsp ground coriander
(cilantro)

40 g/1½ oz/⅓ cup ground nuts

30 ml/2 tbsp oil

6 duck eggs (or size 1 hen
eggs), beaten

4–8 fresh red chillies, seeded
and sliced lengthways into
thin strips

½ handful of fresh coriander
(cilantro)

NOTE *Making egg nets requires some
practice and patience. Instead of a
piping bag, the Thai housewife uses a
bag made of rolled up banana leaf. Or
a gently clenched fist which is dipped
in the egg mixture and then with a
quick movement it is squirted over the
pan with the fingers. From the fingers
the egg mixture slides into four threads
into the pan.*

1 Fry (sauté) the onion and the garlic in the oil until golden.

2 Add the minced meat and stir fry until brown and crumbly. Season with salt, sugar, pepper, soy sauce and coriander.

3 Dry-fry the ground nuts in a frying pan (skillet), stirring, until golden brown. Add to the meat mixture and mash well.

4 Heat oil in a 20 cm/8 in wok or frying pan (skillet). Pour egg into a piping bag fitted with a small plain nozzle. Or a paper piping bag with the fine point snipped off. Squeeze the egg in thin threads into the oil. Guide the bag horizontally and vertically so that a fine, close net is formed. The surface of the net should not be allowed to harden. Take pan off the heat.

5 Now place two to three chilli strips and then three to four coriander leaves in the centre of the net and spread 15–30 ml/ 1–2 tbsp of filling. Fold the net together like an envelope. Transfer the egg net to a plate and keep warm.

6 In this way make 12 to 15 nets.

Fried Prawn Balls

TORD MAN KUNG

PREPARATION TIME: 30 MINUTES
SERVES 4-6

2 spring onions (scallions), roughly chopped

3 garlic cloves, roughly crushed

450 g/1 lb/4 cups peeled prawns (shrimp)

30 ml/2 tbsp fresh chopped coriander (cilantro)

5 ml/1 tsp salt

5 ml/1 tsp pepper

2.5 ml/½ tsp grated nutmeg

1 (size 1) egg

45-60 ml/3-4 tbsp plain (all-purpose) flour

Oil for shallow frying

Fresh coriander to garnish

To serve: Sharp Sauce (see page 28) or Chilli Ginger Sauce (see page 30)

1 Purée the spring onions and garlic with the prawns and the coriander in a blender or food processor.

2 Season the mixture with salt, pepper and nutmeg and blend in the egg and flour to form a firm dough.

3 Heat about 5 mm/¼ in of oil in a frying pan (skillet). Make little balls from the prawn dough and fry (sauté) turning occasionally for about 7 minutes until crisp and golden brown.

4 Drain on kitchen paper, transfer to a serving dish and sprinkle with coriander leaves to garnish. Serve with Sharp Sauce or Chilli Ginger Sauce.

Preserved Vegetables

PAK DONG

PREPARATION TIME: 1 HOUR
SERVES 6-8

½ cucumber

225 g/8 oz/½ lb broccoli, cut in small florets

225 g/8 oz/½ lb cauliflower, cut in small florets

2 carrots, sliced and cut in shapes, if liked

½ small Chinese leaves (stem lettuce), thickly sliced

225g/8 oz/½ lb pak soi or Swiss chard, thickly sliced

200 g/7 oz can sweetcorn (corn), drained

750 ml/1¼ pts/3 cups rice or white wine vinegar

750 ml/1¼ pts/3 cups water

45 ml/3 tbsp sugar

5-10 ml/1-2 tsp salt

10 garlic cloves, crushed

3-4 onions, grated

8-10 small dried chillies, crushed

100 ml/3½ fl oz/6½ tbsp soya or groundnut (peanut) oil

45 ml/3 tbsp toasted sesame seeds

1 Cut off thin strips of cucumber skin all round, using a citrus peeler or a small sharp knife. Cut cucumber into slices.

2 Bring the vinegar, water, sugar and salt to the boil and cook the vegetables in it a portion at a time until just cooked: first the carrots, then the broccoli and cauliflower florets, then the cucumber slices and finally the Chinese leaves, pak soi and the sweetcorn.

3 Mash the garlic, onions and chillies together to a paste.

4 Heat the oil in a large saucepan and stir-fry the paste for 3 minutes. Add the vegetables with the liquid and simmer for 2 minutes.

5 Remove the vegetables with a draining spoon and place on a plate. Sprinkle sesame seeds over and serve warm or cold.

Cucumber and Radish Pickles

TAENG KAW HOA PAK KAD DONG

PREPARATION TIME: 15 MINUTES
PLUS CHILLING TIME
SERVES 6-8

2 cucumbers, cut in matchsticks

1 large winter radish or mouli cut in matchsticks and/or attractively shaped slices

3 shallots or 1 onion, finely chopped

100 ml/3½ fl oz/6½ tbsp white wine vinegar

100 ml/3½ fl oz/6½ tbsp water

5-10 ml/1-2 tsp sugar

2.5 ml/½ tsp cayenne

5 ml/1 tsp salt

1 Put prepared cucumber and radish in a bowl and add the shallots.

2 Mix the vinegar with the water and bring to the boil with the sugar, cayenne and salt.

3 Leave the liquid to cool, then pour over the vegetables. Cover and chill.

These pickles go particularly well with Beef Curry with Creamed Coconut and Potatoes (page 74) and Pork on Rice (page 79).

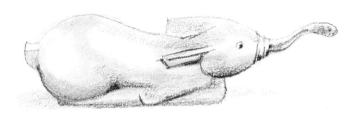

Sweet and Sour Cucumbers

TAENG KWA BRIO WAN

PREPARATION TIME: 15 MINUTES
CHILLING TIME: 1 HOUR
SERVES 6–8

---

2 cucumbers, cut in matchsticks

1 red onion, finely chopped reserving 1 slice for garnish

3–4 dried chillies, crushed

75–90ml/5–6 tbsp white wine vinegar

150 ml/¼ pt/⅔ cup water

75 ml/5 tbsp sugar

5 ml/1 tsp salt

1 Place prepared cucumber in a bowl and sprinkle with the finely chopped onion and the chillies.

2 Bring the vinegar and water to the boil with the sugar and salt and simmer until all the sugar has dissolved.

3 Pour over the cucumber. Leave to cool, cover and chill before serving garnished with reserved slice of onion.

Bean Sprouts with Pork

PAD NUA NGORK

PREPARATION TIME: 20 MINUTES
SERVES 4-6

---

225 g/8 oz/2 cups lean pork cut
  in thin strips

30 ml/2 tbsp oil

5 garlic cloves, crushed

150 g/5 oz/1¼ cups peeled
  prawns (shrimp)

Salt

250 g/9 oz/2¼ cups soya bean
  sprouts

30 ml/2 tbsp fish sauce
  (see page 24)

15 ml/1 tbsp soy sauce

5-10 ml/1-2 tsp sugar

1 Stir-fry pork quickly in the oil in a frying pan (skillet) or a wok to brown.

2 Add the garlic and fry (sauté) for 1 minute.

3 Add the prawns and bean sprouts, stir, reduce heat and cook, stirring for 1 minute. Season with salt, fish sauce, soy sauce and sugar.

COOK'S TIP: Double the ingredients,
add rice and a vegetable
accompaniment and this will make a
main course for 4 people.

Cucumber and Carrot Salad

YAM TAENG KWA

PREPARATION TIME: 20 MINUTES
SERVES 4

1 cucumber

2–3 carrots, thinly sliced

2 red onions, finely chopped

1–2 small fresh red chillies, seeded and sliced thinly

120 ml/4 fl oz/½ cup white wine vinegar

10 ml/2 tsp salt

15–20 ml/3–4 tsp sugar

1 Cut off thin strips of the cucumber skin at intervals all round. Halve lengthways, remove the seeds and slice thinly.

2 Put in a bowl with the carrots, onions and chillies.

3 Mix the vinegar with the salt and sugar. Pour over vegetables and toss well before serving.

Fried Vegetables

BAI GUP KAO

PREPARATION TIME: 20 MINUTES
SERVES 4-6

1 kg/2¼ lb mixed vegetables
(eg cauliflower, Chinese leaves
[stem lettuce], carrots,
bamboo shoots, soya bean
sprouts, winter radish, mouli,
red [bell] peppers, spinach)

45-60 ml/3-4 tbsp oil

8 garlic cloves, crushed

1 onion, halved and sliced

60 ml/4 tbsp fish sauce
(see page 24)

2.5 ml/½ tsp white pepper

1 Cut the vegetables into walnut sized pieces (cauliflower into florets, carrots in slices, bamboo shoots and Chinese leaves etc into small strips).

2 Stir-fry adding one sort of vegetable (say cauliflower) at a time in the oil in a large frying pan (skillet) or wok. When all the vegetables are in, add the onions and the garlic and stir fry for 2 to 3 minutes.

3 Season with fish sauce and pepper, cover and cook for a few minutes. The vegetables should not be too soft.

Papaya Salad

S O M   T A M   M A L A K O R

PREPARATION TIME: 25 MINUTES
PLUS COOLING TIME
SERVES 4

1 unripe, still green papaya

6 garlic cloves, crushed

2 dried chillies, crushed

100 g/4 oz/1 cup chopped
dried prawns (shrimps) or
15 ml/1 tbsp prawn paste
(see page 25)

2.5 ml/½ tsp white pepper

45 ml/3 tbsp fish sauce
(see page 24)

15 ml/1 tbsp tamarind juice
(see page 23)

15 ml/1 tbsp palm or caster
(superfine) sugar

30 ml/2 tbsp lemon juice

2 lemons

2 ripe papayas

1 Halve the unripe papaya, scrape out the seeds (pits). If liked, scoop out a few small balls of flesh, using a melon baller for garnish, then peel the remaining fruit. Chop the flesh and mash in a bowl.

2 Pound the garlic, chillies, prawns and pepper in a pestle and mortar or in a bowl with the end of a rolling pin.

3 Mix the fish sauce with the tamarind juice, sugar and lemon juice and bring to the boil. Cool and stir in spice paste and the mashed papaya.

4 Peel the lemons like apples and completely remove the white pith. Cut the fruit into segments. Finely chop half the segments. Fold into the papaya mixture.

5 Halve ripe papayas and scoop out the seeds (pits). Spoon the papaya and lemon mixture into the cavities. Garnish with lemon segments and papaya balls.

Sharp Beef Salad

YAM NUA YANG

PREPARATION TIME: 20 MINUTES
SERVES 4–6

1 cucumber

8 garlic cloves, crushed

5 fresh red chillies, seeded and
sliced into thin rings

45 ml/3 tbsp fish sauce
(see page 24)

15 ml/1 tbsp lime or lemon
juice

2.5 ml/½ tsp salt

5 ml/1 tsp sugar

Iceberg lettuce leaves

450 g/1 lb cold roast beef in a
piece, cut in thin strips

2 onions, halved and thinly
sliced

COOK'S TIP: *The original recipe for
this salad requires 20 red chillies,
which for most Europeans is too much.
Even 5 chillies make the salad very
fiery so reduce the quantity according
to taste.*

1 Cut half the cucumber into 4
equal pieces. Using a sharp
pointed knife cut through to the
centre of each piece in a zig-zag
pattern all round and pull apart.
Reserve for garnish.

2 Using a citrus peeler or sharp
knife, cut strips of skin off
remaining half cucumber all round
then thinly slice.

3 Mix the garlic, chillies, fish
sauce, lime juice, salt and
sugar well together.

4 Arrange the lettuce leaves on
serving plates, arrange the
meat and some of the cucumber
slices on top. Pour the sauce over.
Garnish with the onion slices,
remaining cucumber slices and
vandyked cucumbers.

King Prawn and Lobster Salad

KUNG MANGKON LI PHAI

PREPARATION TIME: 25 MINUTES
SERVES 2-4

1 fresh pineapple

1 cooked lobster
(about 800 g/1¾ lb)

6 cooked king prawns (jumbo shrimp) with shells

2 oranges

225 g/8 oz/½ lb cooked tiny broccoli florets

Salt

DRESSING:

2 egg yolks

5 ml/1 tsp mustard

Pinch of salt and pepper

100 ml/3½ fl oz/6½ tbsp oil

15 ml/1 tbsp vinegar

15 ml/1 tbsp lime or lemon juice

5 ml/1 tsp sugar

1 Cut the pineapple in half lengthways. Cut out and dice the flesh, discarding any tough central core.

2 Halve the lobster then remove the meat from the pincers and the tail. Cut tail meat into bite-sized pieces.

3 Peel the prawns.

4 Peel the oranges like apples, removing all the white pith. Cut into segments.

5 Mix the diced pineapple together with the lobster, prawns and orange segments and arrange in the scooped out pineapple halves. Dot with broccoli florets. Season with salt.

6 Whisk dressing ingredients together until creamy.

7 Arrange the pineapple halves on plates, and serve the dressing separately.

COOK'S TIPS: *It looks particularly pretty if the sauce is served in small, scooped out pumpkins or squash.*

If serving 4 people, use a large pineapple and cut it in quarters lengthways instead of halves then proceed as above.

Soups

*In most European countries, soups are
usually served at the beginning of the
meal or as a light meal on their own.
But in Thailand they appear on the table
at the same time with all the other foods.
They are really more like stews, with
sometimes quite large pieces of meat,
poultry, vegetables, fish or seafood
simmered in clear liquid.
They are light, fragrant, colourful and
mouthwateringly delicious.*

Spicy Beef Soup

TOM NEUA

PREPARATION TIME: 2 HOURS
SERVES 4–6

450 g/1 lb lean stewing beef, cut in thin strips

750 ml/ 1¼ pts/3 cups water

3 cm/1¼ in piece galgant root, grated or 5 ml/1 tsp ground ginger

2.5 cm/1 in piece fresh root ginger, grated

30 ml/2 tbsp soy sauce

5–10 ml/1–2 tsp salt

1 bay leaf

2.5 cm/1 in piece cinnamon stick

200 g/7 oz/1¾ cups chopped celery

200 g/7 oz/1¾ cups shredded Chinese leaves (stem lettuce)

4 garlic cloves, finely chopped

15 ml/1 tbsp oil

1 Place the meat in a saucepan with the water. Add the galgant, ginger, soy sauce, salt, bay leaf and cinnamon. Bring to the boil, reduce heat, cover and simmer gently for 1½ hours.

2 Add the celery and the Chinese leaves 10 minutes before the end of the cooking time.

3 Fry (sauté) the garlic in the oil until lightly golden. Do not let it brown too much or it will become bitter. Drain on kitchen paper and sprinkle over soup just before serving.

~ 58 ~

Mushroom and Chilli Soup

TOM JAM HED SOT

PREPARATION TIME: 30 MINUTES
SERVES 4

450 g/1 lb button mushrooms

500 ml/17 fl oz/2¼ cups
   coconut milk (see page 18)

Salt

1 small piece lemon grass
   (about 25 g/1 oz/2 tbsp),
   crushed

5 lime or lemon leaves (or use
   lemon balm or mint),
   chopped

Juice of 2 limes or small
   lemons

30–45 ml/2–3 tbsp fish sauce
   (see page 24)

3 small fresh red chillies,
   seeded and sliced into
   thin rings

Fresh coriander (cilantro)
   leaves to garnish

1 Place the mushrooms in a saucepan with the coconut milk. Season lightly with salt.

2 Add the lemon grass, lime leaves, lime juice and fish sauce and cook for about 4 minutes until the mushrooms are cooked, but not too soft.

3 Add the chillies and sprinkle with the coriander leaves just before serving.

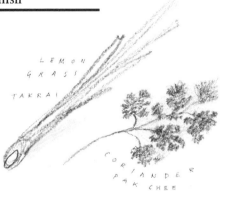

Coconut Soup with Chicken

GAENG KATI KAI

PREPARATION TIME: 40 MINUTES
SERVES 6-8

1.5 litres/2½ pts/6 cups strong chicken stock (see page 26)

1 onion, finely chopped

2 garlic cloves, crushed

1 small piece lemon grass (about 25 g/1 oz/2 tbsp), crushed

3 cm/1¼ in piece galgant root, grated or 5 ml/1 tsp ground ginger

175 g/6 oz/⅓ lb button mushrooms, halved

450 g/1 lb chicken breast fillet, cut in small strips

150 g/5 oz/1¼ cups creamed coconut (Santen, see page 18)

45 ml/3 tbsp lemon juice

45 ml/3 tbsp fish sauce (see page 24)

Salt

4-6 small fresh red and green chillies, seeded and sliced into thin rings

1 Put the chicken stock in a saucepan. Add the onion, garlic, lemon grass and galgant root, bring to the boil and simmer for 15 minutes.

2 Strain, return to saucepan and bring to the boil again.

3 Add the mushrooms, chicken meat and creamed coconut and simmer for 4 minutes.

4 Add the lemon juice and fish sauce and if necessary season with some salt.

5 Place chillies in a small bowl and serve separately to sprinkle over the soup.

Chicken Soup with Radish

KAENG CHOED RUAM MIT

PREPARATION TIME: 40 MINUTES
SERVES 4-6

750 ml/1¼ pts/3 cups chicken stock (see page 26)

350 g/12 oz/3 cups sliced carrots

350 g/12 oz/3 cups sliced winter radish or mouli

225 g/8 oz/½ lb chicken breast fillet, cut in small strips

225 g/8 oz/2 cups chicken livers, cut in thin strips

5 ml/1 tsp white pepper

30 ml/2 tbsp soy sauce or fish sauce (see page 24)

100 g/4 oz/1 cup peeled prawns (shrimp)

1 spring onion (scallion), chopped

Fresh coriander leaves to garnish

1 Bring the chicken stock to the boil. Add the prepared carrots and radish, cover and simmer for 20 minutes.

2 Add the chicken breast and livers and simmer gently for 5 minutes in the hot stock, but do not allow to boil rapidly.

3 Season with pepper and soy or fish sauce. Add the shrimps and spring onion leave to stand for 3 to 4 minutes.

4 Serve garnished with fresh coriander leaves.

Sour Spicy Fish Soup

TOM YAM PLA KAPHONG KHAO

PREPARATION TIME: 40 MINUTES
SERVES 3-4

1 large mullet or dorado
(dolphin fish), about
450 g/1 lb, cleaned and
scaled

600 ml/1 pt/2½ cups fish stock
(see page 27)

5 shallots or 1 large onion,

finely chopped

1 small piece lemon grass
(about 25 g/1 oz/2 tbsp),
crushed

3 cm/1¼ in piece galgant root,
grated or 5 ml/1 tsp ground
ginger

4-6 fresh red chillies, seeded
and sliced into thin rings or
6-8 small dried ones, crushed

grated rind of 5 limes or small
lemons

100 g/4 oz/¼ lb button
mushrooms

30 ml/2 tbsp lime or lemon
juice

30 ml/2 tbsp fish sauce
(see page 24)

45-60 ml/3-4 tbsp coriander
(cilantro) leaves to garnish

1 Rinse the fish and cut into
four to six pieces.

2 Place stock in a saucepan with
the shallots, lemon grass,
galgant root, chillies and lime rind.

3 Cover and simmer for 10
minutes.

4 Add the pieces of fish and the
mushrooms to the stock with
lime juice and fish sauce and
simmer for about 15 minutes.

5 Sprinkle the soup with
coriander leaves before serving.

Sweet and Sour Fish Soup

PLA KABOK TOM SOM

PREPARATION TIME: 20 MINUTES
PLUS MARINATING TIME
SERVES 4

5-6 red mullet (goatfish), about 600 g/1¼ lb in all, cleaned and scaled

2.5 cm/1 in piece fresh root ginger, grated

1 small piece lemon grass (about 25 g/1 oz/2 tbsp) crushed

30 ml/2 tbsp prawn (shrimp) paste (see page 25)

750 ml/1¼ pts/3 cups water

90 ml/6 tbsp tamarind juice (see page 23)

15-30 ml/1-2 tbsp palm or soft brown sugar

30-45 ml/2-3 tbsp fish sauce (see page 24)

2 spring onions (scallions), chopped

3-6 fresh red chillies, seeded and sliced into thin rings

Fresh coriander (cilantro) leaves to garnish

1 Rinse the fish and pat dry with kitchen paper.

2 Crush the ginger with the lemon grass in a pestle and mortar or in a bowl with the end of a rolling pin and add the prawn paste. Rub this mixture into the fish and leave for 1 hour.

3 Bring the water to the boil in a saucepan, add the fish and season the stock with tamarind juice, sugar and fish sauce. Cover and simmer gently for 10 minutes.

4 Add the spring onions and chillies and serve very hot garnished with coriander leaves.

Sweet and Salty Fish Soup

TOM PLA TUSAD

PREPARATION TIME: 1 HOUR
SERVES 4

4 small cleaned mackerel or large sardines

750 ml/1¼ pts/3 cups water

60 ml/4 tbsp soy sauce

5 ml/1 tsp salt

15 ml/1 tbsp palm or light brown sugar

4 garlic cloves, finely chopped

45 ml/3 tbsp oil

5–10ml/1–2 tsp white pepper

60 ml/4 tbsp tamarind juice (see page 23)

Coriander (cilantro) leaves to garnish

1 Cut the heads and tails off fish. Rinse everything under running water. Place the heads and tails in a saucepan, cover with the water and bring to the boil. Half-cover with a lid, reduce heat and simmer gently for 30 minutes.

2 Strain the liquid and discard the head and tails.

3 Return stock to pan and stir in the soy sauce, salt and sugar.

4 Fry (sauté) the garlic in 15 ml/ 1 tbsp of the oil until golden in a small frying pan (skillet). Add the pepper and stir this mixture into the fish stock.

5 Add the tamarind juice and the fish to the stock and cook over a gentle heat for about 15 minutes until fish is cooked but still holds its shape. Sprinkle with coriander leaves before serving.

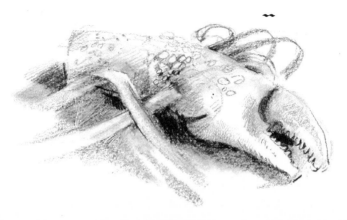

Fresh Mackerel Soup

T O M   P L A

PREPARATION TIME: 45 MINUTES
SERVES 4

2 cleaned mackerel
(heads removed)

5 shallots or 1-2 onions, finely
chopped

Pinch of black pepper

15 ml/1 tbsp prawn (shrimp)
paste (see page 25)

30 ml/2 tbsp chopped
coriander (cilantro)

750 ml/1¼ pts/3 cups water

2.5cm/1 in piece fresh root
ginger, grated

45 ml/3 tbsp tamarind juice
(see page 23)

30 ml/2 tbsp palm or
granulated sugar

45 ml/3 tbsp fish sauce
(see page 24)

5 spring onions (scallions),
chopped

1 Chop each mackerel into five
or six pieces.

2 Mix the shallots with the
pepper, prawn paste and half
the coriander. Mix this paste with
the water in a saucepan and bring
to the boil.

3 Add the ginger, the tamarind
juice, the sugar and the fish
sauce to the saucepan. When the
soup is boiling, add the mackerel
pieces, cover and cook for 10
minutes or until fish is just cooked
but still holds its shape. Add the
spring onions and simmer for 1
minute more.

4 Serve garnished with
remaining coriander.

Fish Soup with Pak Soi

KAENG SONG PRIK SOD KAB PLA

PREPARATION TIME: 40 MINUTES
SERVES 4-6

CHILLI PASTE:

3 dried red chillies, crushed

5 shallots or 1-2 onions, finely chopped

5 garlic cloves, crushed

5 ml/1 tsp salt

15 ml/1 tbsp prawn (shrimp) paste (see page 25)

1 litre/1¾ pts/4¼ cups fish stock (see page 27)

450 g/1 lb pak soi, Swiss chard or Chinese leaves (stem lettuce), roughly chopped

5 small ripe tomatoes, cut in wedges

450 g/1 lb fish fillet, skinned and diced

15 ml/1 tbsp lemon juice

45 ml/3 tbsp fish sauce (see page 24)

A few small wedges of tomato to garnish

1 To make the chilli paste simply mix all ingredients well together, or, for a finer texture, pound in a pestle and mortar or in a bowl with the end of a rolling pin.

2 Bring the fish stock to the boil in a saucepan. Add the chilli paste and the Pak Soi and simmer gently for 10 minutes.

3 Add the tomatoes and fish fillets, season with lemon juice and fish sauce and cook for a further 10 minutes. Serve hot garnished with a few wedges of tomato.

Sour Spicy King Prawn Soup

TOM JAM KUNG

PREPARATION TIME: 25 MINUTES
SERVES 4

8 king prawns (jumbo shrimp) with shells

750 ml/1¼ pts/3 cups chicken stock (see page 26)

2–3 pieces fresh lemon grass, crushed

2.5 cm/1 in piece fresh galgant root, grated or 5 ml/1 tsp ground ginger

100 g/4 oz/¼ lb button mushrooms, halved

1 fresh red chilli, seeded and cut into thin rings

30 ml/2 tbsp fish sauce (see page 24)

30 ml/2 tbsp lime or lemon juice

5 lemon, lemon balm or lemon mint leaves

5–10 ml/1–2 tsp roasted chilli paste (see page 36)

Salt

1 Peel the king prawns but leave the tail fins on. Remove the dark veins down the backs.

2 Bring the chicken stock to the boil, stir in all the ingredients except the prawns and simmer for 2–3 minutes.

3 Finally add the king prawns and cook for a further 3–5 minutes. Season with salt, if liked, remove the lemon grass and lemon leaves and serve the soup very hot.

Soup with Prawns and Sweetcorn

GAENG CHUD KAOPOT AUN

PREPARATION TIME: 15 MINUTES
SERVES 4

4 shallots or 1 onion, finely chopped

45 ml/3 tbsp oil

3 garlic cloves, crushed

750 ml/1¼ pts/3 cups chicken stock (see page 26)

350 g/12 oz/3 cups peeled prawns (shrimp) or crab meat

8 small baby sweetcorn cobs (fresh or drained, canned)

45 ml/3 tbsp fish sauce (see page 24)

Salt

5 ml/1 tsp white pepper

2 eggs, beaten

Coriander (cilantro) leaves to garnish

1 Fry (sauté) the shallots in the hot oil until lightly golden. Add the garlic and stir-fry until golden but not too brown.

2 Add the chicken stock and bring to the boil. Add the prawns and sweetcorn cobs and season the soup with fish sauce, salt and pepper. Simmer for 3 minutes.

3 Gently pour beaten eggs into the soup through the prongs of a fork. Stir gently and sprinkle the soup with coriander leaves to garnish before serving.

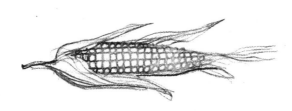

Sour Prawn Soup

TOM KUNG

PREPARATION TIME: 30 MINUTES
SERVES 4

450 g/1 lb/fresh prawns
(shrimp) with shells

6 shallots or 2 onions, finely
chopped

750 ml/1¼ pts/3 cups fish
stock (see page 27)

45 ml/3 tbsp tamarind juice
(see page 23)

2 fresh red chillies, seeded
and cut into thin rings

30 ml/2 tbsp fish sauce
(see page 24)

Whole red chillies to garnish

*COOK'S TIP: Try using soaked salt
cod instead of prawns (see also Rice
Noodles with Fish Sauce page 138).*

1 Shell the prawns and remove
the black veins from down the
backs. Halve diagonally if large, or
leave whole.

2 Put the shallots in a saucepan
with the fish stock, add the
prawns and leave to simmer gently
for 10 minutes.

3 Stir in the tamarind juice and
chillies and season with the
fish sauce. Serve hot, garnished
with whole red chillies.

Meat Dishes

*Beef, pork and poultry are all used
extensively in Thai cooking.
Steamed, fried, roasted or boiled, any
number of dishes can be be prepared with
an enormous variety of colourful
ingredients.
Usually the meat is cut into strips or
pieces and often marinated before
cooking.
Plain boiled rice is always served as an
accompaniment.*

Beef Curry

GAENG NEUA

PREPARATION TIME: 30 MINUTES
SERVES 4

SPICE PASTE:

5 small dried chillies, crushed

5 shallots or 2 small onions, finely chopped

10 garlic cloves, crushed

15 ml/1 tbsp finely chopped lemon grass

15 ml/1 tbsp grated galgant root (or 5 ml/1 tsp ground ginger)

5 ml/1 tsp grated lime or lemon rind

15 ml/1 tbsp ground coriander (cilantro)

Pinch of black pepper

5 ml/1 tsp salt

5 ml/1 tsp prawn (shrimp) paste (see page 25)

30 ml/2 tbsp oil

450 g/1 lb fillet or lean rump or sirloin steak, cut in thin strips

250 ml/8 fl oz/1 cup coconut milk

2 lime leaves or strip of lime or lemon rind

30 ml/2 tbsp fish sauce (see page 24)

30 ml/2 tbsp palm or light brown sugar

Handful of horapa or basil leaves, chopped

1 Pound all the ingredients for the spice paste, except the oil in a pestle and mortar or in a bowl with the end of a rolling pin.

2 Heat the oil in a saucepan and fry (sauté) the paste for about 2 minutes, stirring.

3 Add the steak to the saucepan and stir-fry in the paste for 5 minutes.

4 Add the coconut milk and the lime leaves or rind and leave to simmer uncovered for about 10 minutes. Thin with a little water if necessary. Remove the lime leaves or rind.

5 Season with the fish sauce and the sugar. Stir in the horapa and serve straight away.

Beef Curry with Aubergines and Peppers

GAENG PED NEUA MAKEUA

PREPARATION TIME: 40 MINUTES
SERVES 4

1 aubergine (eggplant), diced

600 g/1¼ lb lean rump steak, cut in thin strips

60 ml/4 tbsp oil

1 green (bell) pepper, seeded and cut in strips

1 red (bell) pepper, seeded and cut in strips

Salt

15 ml/1 tbsp chopped lemon grass

5 ml/1 tsp sambal oelek (see page 25)

250 ml/8 fl oz/1 cup beef stock

Juice of ½ lemon

45 ml/3 tbsp sweet soy sauce (ketjap manis)

15 ml/1 tbsp palm or light brown sugar

½ handful of horapa or basil leaves, chopped

60 ml/4 tbsp desiccated (shredded) coconut

1 Soak the diced aubergine in cold water until ready to use.

2 Fry (sauté) the meat quickly in the oil to brown in a large frying pan (skillet).

3 Add the peppers and the drained aubergines, season with salt, lemon grass and sambal oelek, stir fry for 10 minutes.

4 Add the stock, the lemon juice, soy sauce and sugar and cook for 10 minutes stirring occasionally.

5 Mix in the horapa leaves and sprinkle with coconut. Serve hot.

Beef Curry with Creamed Coconut and Potatoes

GAENG MASAMAN

PREPARATION TIME: 2 HOURS
SERVES 4

CURRY PASTE:

2 onions, finely chopped

10 garlic cloves, crushed

2.5 cm/1 in piece fresh root ginger, grated

30 ml/2 tbsp oil

1 piece lemon grass (about 15 g/½ oz/1 tbsp), crushed or 15 ml/1 tbsp grated lemon rind

1 piece galgant root (about 15 g/½ oz/1 tbsp), grated or 5 ml/1 tsp ground ginger

15 ml/1 tbsp ground coriander (cilantro)

15 ml/1 tbsp ground cross caraway or cumin

15 ml/1 tbsp paprika

5 ml/1 tsp curry powder or garam masala

5 ml/1 tsp salt

600 g/1¼ lb lean beef top rump, cut in thin strips

75 g/3 oz/¾ cup creamed coconut (Santen; see page 18)

200 ml/7 fl oz/scant 1 cup water

4–5 potatoes diced or made into balls with a melon baller

1 large onion, finely chopped for garnish

To serve: Cucumber and Radish Pickles (page 49)

1 Fry (sauté) the onion and the garlic in half the oil until golden brown. Add remaining paste ingredients except lemon grass and galgant root and fry for 2 minutes.

2 Add the lemon grass and galgant root to the paste.

3 Melt the creamed coconut in the water in a large saucepan.

4 Add the curry paste, the meat and the potatoes, season with salt and bring to the boil.

5 Reduce heat, cover and simmer for about 45 minutes to 1 hour. If the sauce becomes too thick, add a little water.

6 Meanwhile fry (sauté) the onion for garnish in the remaining oil until golden brown. Arrange the beef curry in a bowl and sprinkle the fried onion on top. Serve with Cucumber and Radish Pickles.

Red Beef Curry

GAEN PED NEUA

PREPARATION TIME: 1 HOUR
SERVES 4

800 g/1¾ lb lean beef top
rump, cut in thin strips

1 onion, halved and sliced

1 litre/1¾ pts/4¼ cups coconut
milk (see page 18)

5–10 ml/1–2 tsp salt

30 ml/2 tbsp red spice paste
(see page 34)

3 lemon leaves or a piece of
lemon rind

1 small piece lemon grass
(about 10 g/¼ oz/2 tsp)
crushed

30 ml/2 tbsp fish sauce
(see page 24)

2 red (bell) peppers, seeded
and cut in strips

A few horapa or basil leaves
and coriander (cilantro)
leaves to garnish

1 Put everything except the
peppers, horapa and coriander
leaves in a large saucepan and
bring to the boil.

2 Partly cover, reduce heat and
simmer gently for about 45
minutes, stirring from time to time
until meat is tender.

3 Add the peppers and simmer
uncovered for a further 10
minutes or until the sauce has
reduced a little.

4 Place the curry in a bowl and
sprinkle with horapa and
coriander leaves.

Fried Ribs with Pineapple and Chilli

SEE KHRONG MOO SUPPAROT

PREPARATION TIME: 1½ HOURS
SERVES 4

1.5 kg/3 lb pork spare ribs

Salt and pepper

Flour for dusting

Oil for frying

1 small pineapple

300 ml/½ pt/1¼ cups unsweetened pineapple juice

100 ml/3½ fl oz/6½ tbsp water

30 ml/2 tbsp light soy sauce

30 ml/2 tbsp red wine vinegar

15 ml/1 tbsp palm or light brown sugar

2 fresh red chillies, seeded and cut into thin rings

COOK'S TIP: Instead of fresh pineapple use a 350 g/12 oz can in natural juice. Use the juice as part of the amount needed in the recipe.

1 Dust the ribs with seasoned flour, then fry (sauté) in a little oil on all sides until browned. Drain on kitchen paper and place in a large saucepan.

2 Cut off the stalk and the top of the pineapple, place the fruit upright on a plate and cut away the skin generously all round, at the same time removing the brown 'eyes'. Halve the pineapple, quarter and cut out the core. Cut the fruit into walnut sized pieces.

3 Mix the pineapple juice with the water, the soy sauce, the vinegar and the sugar and add to the ribs. Bring to the boil, cover and cook for about 45 minutes. Then remove lid and cook for a further 15 minutes until the sauce is reduced and syrupy.

4 Add the diced pineapple 5 minutes before the end.

5 Sprinkle the chillies over the ribs just before serving.

Grilled Pork

M O O D A E N G

PREPARATION TIME: 1 HOUR
PLUS MARINATING TIME
SERVES 4

1 kg/2¼ lb piece lean pork
shoulder, rind removed

MARINADE:

45 ml/3 tbsp light soy sauce

45 ml/3 tbsp sherry

30 ml/2 tbsp oil (preferably
sesame)

60–75 ml/4–5 tbsp sugar

5 ml/1 tsp salt

5 ml/1 tsp ground ginger

5 ml/1 tsp garlic powder

45 ml/3 tbsp clear honey

Slices of tomato and cucumber
to garnish

1 Cut the pork into slices about
3×5×5 cm/1¼×2×2 in wide.

2 Mix together all the ingredients for the marinade. Rub it
into the meat and then leave to
marinate for 6 hours.

3 Finally grill the meat for about
30 minutes, turning often and
brushing with marinade.

4 Cut the meat into thin slices
and garnish with slices of
cucumber and tomato.

*COOK'S TIP: The meat can be
roasted, turning frequently, in an
ovenproof dish in a very hot oven
240°C/475°F/gas mark 9.*

Red Pork

MOO TORD

PREPARATION TIME: 1¼ HOURS
PLUS MARINATING TIME
SERVES 4

---

100 g/4 oz/½ cup tomato purée
(paste)

Water

90 ml/6 tbsp soy sauce

5 ml/1 tsp salt

40 ml/ 8 tsp sugar

600 g/1¼ lb piece lean pork
shoulder, cut in small strips,
rind removed

30 ml/2 tbsp oil

½ cucumber, peeled, halved
lengthways and sliced

2–4 fresh red chillies, seeded
and diced

30 ml/2 tbsp red wine vinegar

A few coriander (cilantro)
leaves

1 Make the tomato purée up to
400 ml/14 fl oz/1¾ cups with
water. Mix with 60 ml/4 tbsp of
the soy sauce, the salt and 30 ml/
6 tsp of the sugar, add the meat,
toss well and leave to marinate for
2 hours turning occasionally.

2 Bring the meat to the boil in
the marinade, cover, reduce
heat and simmer gently for 30
minutes. Carefully take meat out
of the liquid, drain on kitchen
paper and leave to cool. Reserve
the marinade.

3 Fry (sauté) the meat in the oil
in a frying pan (skillet) for
about 20 minutes on all sides until
crisp and brown. Add the
marinade and boil for about 10
minutes stirring several times until
the sauce is well reduced.

4 Place the meat in a serving
dish, arrange cucumber slices
all round and sprinkle with the
diced chillies and coriander leaves.
Mix the remaining soy sauce with
the vinegar and remaining sugar.
Pour into a small bowl and hand
separately.

Pork on Rice

KAO KHA MOO

PREPARATION TIME: 2 HOURS
SERVES 4

800 g/1¾ lb knuckle of pork

5 garlic cloves, chopped

5 ml/1 tsp aniseed seeds

5 ml/1 tsp ground coriander (cilantro)

5 ml/1 tsp salt

45–60 ml/3–4 tbsp soy sauce

350 g/12 oz/1½ cups long-grain rice

Cucumber slices and coriander (cilantro) leaves to garnish

To serve: Cucumber and Radish Pickles (page 49)

COOK'S TIP: If you find knuckle of pork too fatty, use shoulder instead.

1 Place the knuckle of pork in a saucepan and just cover with water. Add the garlic, aniseed, coriander, salt and soy sauce. Bring to the boil, reduce heat, cover and simmer the knuckle of pork for about 1½ hours.

2 Remove the meat from the liquid and cut into eight pieces and keep warm. Remove the fat from the stock. Then measure a scant 600 ml/1 pt/2½ cups (add water, if necessary) and cook the rice in it for 15 minutes until just tender.

3 Make a ring of the rice on a serving plate and arrange the pieces of meat in the centre. Garnish with cucumber and coriander and serve with pickles.

Pork with Chilli Paste and Green Beans

GAENG PED MOO KAB TUA

PREPARATION TIME: 45 MINUTES
SERVES 4

CHILLI PASTE:

3 dried red chillies, seeded and crushed

6 shallots or 2 onions, finely chopped

5 garlic cloves, crushed

2.5 ml/½ tsp grated galgant root (or ground ginger)

Pinch of black pepper

15 ml/1 tbsp finely chopped lemon grass

15 ml/1 tbsp ground coriander (cilantro)

5 ml/1 tsp grated lime or lemon rind

Salt

5 ml/1 tsp prawn (shrimp) paste (see page 25)

800 g/1¾ lb lean pork, cut in small strips

60 ml/4 tbsp soy sauce

350 g/12 oz/¾ lb green beans, cut in pieces

45–60 ml/3–4 tbsp oil

15 ml/1 tbsp palm or soft brown sugar

2 fresh red chillies, seeded and cut in thin rings

1 Pound all the ingredients for the chilli paste in a pestle and mortar or in a bowl with the end of a rolling pin.

2 Toss the meat in 30 ml/2 tbsp of the soy sauce.

3 Cook the beans in lightly salted boiling water until just tender, then drain.

4 Heat all but 15 ml/1 tbsp of the oil in a frying pan (skillet) and fry (sauté) the meat quickly to brown. Remove with a draining spoon.

5 Stir-fry the curry paste in the remaining oil for 2 minutes, then add the meat, the sugar, the remaining 30 ml/2 tbsp soy sauce and the green beans. Mix well.

6 Sprinkle the fresh chillies over the dish before serving.

Sweet and Sour Pork

M O O   B R I O   W A N

PREPARATION TIME: 2 HOURS
PLUS MARINATING TIME
SERVES 4

1.25 kg/2¾ lb piece pork shoulder, cut in small strips

MARINADE:

60 ml/4 tbsp soy sauce

45 ml/3 tbsp rice wine or dry sherry

5 ml/1 tsp salt

5 ml/1 tsp white pepper

5 ml/1 tsp ground ginger

SWEET AND SOUR SAUCE:

200 ml/7 fl oz/scant 1 cup unsweetened pineapple juice (including juice from can of pineapple, see below)

100 ml/3½ fl oz/6½ tbsp tomato ketchup (catsup)

2.5 cm/1 in piece fresh root ginger, grated

30 ml/2 tbsp red wine vinegar

30 ml/2 tbsp sugar

2.5 ml/½ tsp salt

400 ml/14 fl oz/1¾ cups pork or beef stock

TO FINISH:

30 ml/2 tbsp oil

1 onion, cut into rings

4 fresh red chillies, seeded and cut into thin rings

1 green (bell) pepper, cut in neat pieces

1 red (bell) pepper, cut in neat pieces

250 g/9 oz/good 2 cups drained canned or fresh pineapple pieces

1 Place the pork in a dish.

2 Mix the marinade ingredients together and pour over the meat. Leave to marinate for 3 hours, turning occasionally.

3 Mix the sweet and sour sauce ingredients together.

4 Heat half the oil in a large pan. Add the marinated pork and fry (sauté) quickly on all sides to brown. Add the sweet and sour sauce, bring to the boil reduce heat, half cover and simmer for 1 to 1¼ hours.

5 Fry the onion rings in the remaining oil until soft but not brown. Add the peppers and chillies and stir fry for 2 minutes. Add these ingredients and pineapple pieces to the meat and heat through. Serve hot.

Sweet Pork

MOO WAN

PREPARATION TIME: 2 HOURS
SERVES 4-6

750 ml/1¼ pts/3 cups water

150 g/5 oz/⅔ cup soft dark brown sugar (or ½ sugar, ½ molasses)

150 ml/¼ pt/⅔ cup soy sauce

150 ml/¼ pt/⅔ cup fish sauce (see page 24)

1 kg/2¼ lb lean pork shoulder, without rind

2 onions, finely chopped, reserving 1 slice for garnish

45 ml/3 tbsp oil

1 Mix the water with the sugar or sugar and molasses, the soy and fish sauces in a saucepan.

2 Add the meat and bring to the boil. Reduce heat, half cover and simmer for about 1¼ hours, turning the meat several times and spooning the stock over it (the stock should reduce by at least half).

3 Take the meat out of the stock and place in a warm serving dish. Keep warm.

4 Fry (sauté) the onions in the oil until golden brown.

5 Slice the meat. Spoon the sauce over, sprinkle the fried onions on top and garnish with the reserved raw onion.

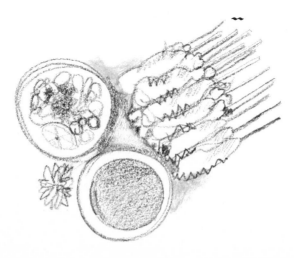

Pork with Prawns

GAENG MOO SA

PREPARATION TIME: 30 MINUTES
SERVES 4

600 ml/1 pt/2½ cups coconut milk (see page 18)

600g/1¼lb pork fillet, cut in thin slices

5 ml/1 tsp salt

5 ml/1 tsp sugar

5 ml/1 tsp roasted chilli paste (see page 36) or red spice paste (see page 34)

200 g/7 oz/1¾ cups peeled prawns (shrimp)

2-3 fresh red chillies, seeded and cut in thin strips

Coriander (cilantro) leaves to garnish

1 Heat the coconut milk in a large pan and simmer for 2 to 3 minutes.

2 Add the meat, salt, sugar and chilli or spice paste and simmer for about 20 minutes.

3 Add the prawns and cook a further 5 minutes. The coconut milk should now be quite thick. Transfer to a warm dish and sprinkle with chilli strips and coriander before serving.

Kidneys with Mushrooms

TAI PAD HED

PREPARATION TIME: 20 MINUTES
PLUS SOAKING TIME
SERVES 3–4

450 g/1 lb pig's kidneys, halved lengthways and cores removed

6 dried tongu (shiitake) mushrooms

1 onion, finely chopped

2 garlic cloves, crushed

45–60 ml/3–4 tbsp oil

60 ml/4 tbsp soy sauce

30 ml/2 tbsp commercial chilli sauce

Coriander (cilantro) leaves to garnish

1 Soak the kidneys in cold water for 3 to 4 hours, changing the water several times.

2 Dry on kitchen paper then cut into bite-sized pieces.

3 Meanwhile soak the mushrooms in lukewarm water for about 15 minutes. Drain, reserving the water, discard stalks and cut caps into thin strips.

4 Fry (sauté) the onion in the oil in a frying pan (skillet) until golden. Add the garlic and the kidneys and fry quickly to brown.

5 Add the mushrooms, the soy sauce, chilli sauce and 60 ml/ 4 tbsp of the mushroom water and cook gently, stirring for 3 to 4 minutes. Do not let the kidneys become hard. Serve garnished with coriander leaves.

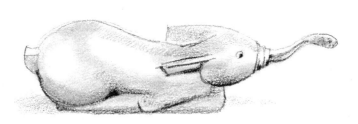

Chicken with Ginger and Mushrooms

KAI KING

PREPARATION TIME: 40 MINUTES
SERVES 4-6

8 dried tongu (shiitake) mushrooms

1 onion, finely chopped

45 ml/3 tbsp oil

4 garlic cloves, crushed

1 kg/2¼ lb chicken breast, cut in bite-sized pieces

2-3 spring onions (scallions), sliced

4 cm/1½ in piece fresh root ginger, grated

3-6 fresh red chillies, seeded and sliced into thin rings

45 ml/3 tbsp soy sauce

30 ml/2 tbsp chopped mint

15 ml/1 tbsp sugar

30-45 ml/2-3 tbsp fish sauce (see page 24)

30 ml/2 tbsp rice or white wine vinegar

Salt if necessary

Sprigs of mint to garnish

1 Soak the mushrooms for about 15 minutes in lukewarm water. Drain, reserving water. Discard stalks and cut caps into thin strips.

2 Meanwhile, fry (sauté) the onion in the oil in a large frying pan (skillet) until golden. Add the garlic and fry for 1 minute. Remove and place on one side.

3 Add chicken to frying pan and stir-fry quickly to seal. Return onion mixture to the pan.

4 Add the mushrooms, spring onions, ginger, chillies, soy sauce and mint. Stir-fry for 5 minutes. Add 60 ml/4 tbsp of the mushroom water. Season with sugar, fish sauce, rice vinegar and some salt if necessary and simmer for 3-4 minutes. Serve hot garnished with sprigs of mint.

Chicken in Peanut Sauce

KAI TUA

PREPARATION TIME: 40 MINUTES
PLUS MARINATING TIME
SERVES 4

SPICE PASTE:

2.5 cm/1 in piece fresh root
ginger, grated

4 garlic cloves, crushed

5 ml/1 tsp ground coriander
(cilantro)

5 ml/1 tsp ground cross
caraway or cumin

2.5 ml/½ tsp each of salt and pepper

Pinch of cinnamon

Pinch of ground cloves

800 g/1¾ lb chicken breast, cut
in bite-sized pieces

225 g/8 oz/½ lb broccoli florets or
green beans, cut in three pieces

1 large onion, finely chopped

45 ml/3 tbsp oil

4 spring onions (scallions),
sliced

4–6 dried chillies, crushed

75 g/3 oz/¾ cup unsalted
peanuts, toasted and ground

250 ml/8 fl oz/1 cup coconut
milk (see page 18)

15 ml/1 tbsp sugar

30–45 ml/2–3 tbsp soy sauce

1 Pound all the spice paste
ingredients together with a
pestle and mortar or in a bowl
with the end of a rolling pin. Rub
into the meat and leave to stand
for 1 hour.

2 Cook the broccoli or beans in
lightly salted boiling water
until just tender. Drain and rinse
with cold water.

3 Fry (sauté) the onion in the oil
in a large frying pan (skillet) or
wok until golden, then add the
broccoli or the beans, the spring
onions and the chillies and stir-fry
for 2 to 3 minutes.

4 Remove the vegetables or
push to one side and fry the
chicken meat on all sides. Mix
with the vegetables and cover in
the coconut milk.

5 Add the sugar, soy sauce and
peanuts and season the dish
with salt to taste. Cook for a
further 5 minutes stirring
frequently. Serve immediately.

Chicken Curry with Horapa or Basil Leaves

GAENG KEO WAN KAI

PREPARATION TIME: 40 MINUTES
SERVES 4

800 g/1¾ lb chicken breast, cut in thin strips

600 ml/1 pt/2½ cups coconut milk (see page 18)

5 ml/1 tsp salt

2.5 cm/1 in piece galgant root (or 5 ml/1 tsp ground ginger)

30 ml/2 tbsp green spice paste (see page 35)

5 lemon leaves or a piece of lemon rind

2 long fresh green chillies, seeded and cut in thin strips or use 1 green (bell) pepper, seeded and cut in thin strips and 4 dried chillies, crushed

100 g/4 oz/¼ lb small makeur or aubergine (eggplant), diced small

10 horapa or basil leaves

1 Put the chicken meat in a pan with the coconut milk. Bring to the boil and cook for 5 minutes, remove meat with a draining spoon and place on one side.

2 Add the salt, galgant root or ground ginger, spice paste, lemon leaves or rind and the chillies.

3 Bring to the boil again, reduce heat and simmer uncovered for 20 minutes.

4 Add the chicken meat and the makeur or aubergine and simmer gently for 5 minutes or until makeur is tender but still holds its shape. Remove the lemon leaves or rind, pour the curry into a bowl and garnish with the horapa or basil leaves.

Chicken in Sauce

KAO RAD NA KAI

PREPARATION TIME: 1 HOUR
PLUS MARINATING TIME
SERVES 4

450 g/1 lb chicken leg or thigh meat, skinned and cut in bite-sized pieces

225 g/8 oz/2 cups chicken livers, trimmed and cut in bite-sized pieces

75 ml/5 tbsp soy sauce

3 dried tongu (shiitake) mushrooms

60 ml/4 tbsp oil

1 onion, finely chopped

4 garlic cloves, crushed

225 g/8 oz/2 cups sliced carrots, cut in attractive shapes if liked

225 g/8 oz/½ lb broccoli stalks, trimmed and sliced (reserve florets for another recipe)

200 ml/7 fl oz/scant 1 cup chicken stock (see page 26)

Salt and white pepper

15 ml/1 tbsp sugar

15 ml/1 tbsp cornflour (cornstarch)

SAUCE:

4-8 dried chillies, crushed

90 ml/6 tbsp red wine vinegar

1 Toss the chicken meat and livers in 30 ml/2 tbsp of the soy sauce and marinate for about 1 hour.

2 Soak the mushrooms in lukewarm water for about 15 minutes. Drain, reserving the water. Discard stalks and cut caps into small strips.

3 Heat the oil in a large frying pan (skillet) and soften the onion. Add the carrots and broccoli stalks and stir-fry for 2 minutes. Then add the chicken meat (not the liver) and the garlic and stir-fry for 3–4 minutes.

4 Cover in the chicken stock and season with the remaining soy sauce, salt, pepper and sugar. Add the tongu mushrooms and 45 ml/ 3 tbsp of the soaking water. Cover and simmer for about 30 minutes, until the meat and the vegetables are tender.

5 Add the chicken livers for last 5 minutes of the cooking time.

6 Mix the cornflour with 45 ml/ 3 tbsp of water and add to the sauce. Bring to the boil, stirring until the sauce thickens. Turn into a serving dish.

7 Mix the crushed chillies with the vinegar and pour into a small bowl and serve with the chicken.

Chicken with Water Chestnuts

KAI GUP KAO LAD

PREPARATION TIME: 20 MINUTES
SERVES 4

SPICE PASTE:

2 shallots or 1 small onion, finely chopped

5 garlic cloves, crushed

2.5 ml/½ tsp black pepper

15 ml/1 tbsp ground coriander (cilantro)

45 ml/3 tbsp oil

450 g/1 lb chicken breast, cut in bite-sized pieces

150 g/5 oz/1¼ cups chicken livers, cut in bite-sized pieces

500 ml/17 fl oz/2¼ cups chicken stock (see page 26)

225 g/8 oz/½ lb can water chestnuts, drained and halved

15 ml/1 tbsp palm or granulated sugar

Salt

Coriander (cilantro) leaves to garnish

1 Pound the shallots and the garlic with the pepper and coriander in a pestle and mortar or in a bowl with the end of a rolling pin.

2 Heat the oil in a large saucepan or wok and fry (sauté) the spice paste for 2 to 3 minutes, stirring.

3 Add the chicken breast and the livers and stir-fry for 2 minutes. Pour in the stock and simmer for about 5 minutes.

4 Add the water chestnuts, the sugar and a little salt if necessary. Cook for a further 2 to 3 minutes. Garnish with coriander leaves.

Chicken with Peppers

PAD PED KAI

PREPARATION TIME: 30 MINUTES
SERVES 4

4 garlic cloves, crushed

8 horapa or basil leaves, chopped

60 ml/4 tbsp oil

800 g/1¾ lb chicken breast, cut in small strips

5 spring onions (scallions), sliced

½ each of red and green (bell) peppers

4 fresh red chillies, seeded and cut into thin rings

75 ml/5 tbsp fish sauce (see page 24)

Salt

A few horapa or basil leaves to garnish

1 Pound the garlic with the chopped horapa or basil leaves in a pestle and mortar or in a bowl with the end of a rolling pin.

2 Heat the oil in a frying pan (skillet). Fry (sauté) the meat, the garlic paste, the spring onions, the peppers and the chillies for 3 minutes without browning. Cover and cook gently for about 5 minutes.

3 Season with the fish sauce and salt as required and sprinkle basil leaves on top.

Chicken in Coconut Milk

DOM KA KAI

PREPARATION TIME: 3 HOURS
SERVES 4

1 oven-ready (broiler) chicken about 1.5 kg/3 lb, cut in 4–6 pieces

8 pieces dried galgant root (each 1 cm/½ in long)

750 ml/1¼ pts/3 cups coconut milk (see page 18)

2.5 ml/½ tsp salt

2.5 ml/½ tsp white pepper

2.5 ml/½ tsp ground coriander (cilantro)

Grated rind of 1 lime or ½ lemon

2.5 ml/½ tsp finely chopped lemon grass

4 lemon or lime leaves (or lemon balm or mint)

50 g/2 oz/½ cup creamed coconut (Santen; see page 18)

30 ml/2 tbsp soy sauce

30–45 ml/2–3 tbsp lime or lemon juice

Chopped coriander (cilantro) to garnish

1 Place the chicken pieces in a wok or large saucepan. Add the galgant root, the coconut milk, salt, pepper, coriander, lime peel, lemon grass and leaves.

2 Bring to the boil reduce heat and simmer uncovered for about 40 minutes until the chicken is tender and the liquid has reduced by about half. Stir and turn the chicken pieces often.

3 Add the creamed coconut, the soy sauce and the lime juice, and simmer for a further 15 minutes. Thin the sauce with a little water if necessary.

4 Remove the lime or lemon leaves and sprinkle with chopped coriander to garnish.

Marinated Chicken Legs with Vegetables and Mushrooms

NONG KAI KAB PAK KAB HED

PREPARATION TIME: 1¾ HOURS
PLUS MARINATING
SERVES 4

45 ml/3 tbsp sweet soy sauce (ketjab manis)

5 ml/1 tsp sambal oelek (see page 25)

4 chicken leg portions

40 g/1½ oz/3 tbsp dried mu-err (Chinese cloud ear) mushrooms

40 g/1½ oz/3 tbsp dried tongu (shiitake) mushrooms

Oil for deep or shallow frying

150 g/5 oz/1¼ cups soya bean sprouts (fresh or drained canned)

150 g/5 oz/1¼ cups canned bamboo shoots, chopped

100 g/4 oz/1 cup chopped celery

100 g/4 oz/1 cup sliced carrots, cut in attractive shapes if liked

30 ml/2 tbsp fish sauce (see page 24)

30 ml/2 tbsp oyster sauce

30 ml/2 tbsp palm or soft brown sugar

salt

Coriander (cilantro) leaves to garnish

1 Mix the soy sauce and sambal oelek and rub into the chicken legs. Leave to marinate in the fridge for at least 5 hours.

2 Soak the two types of mushrooms separately in lukewarm water: the mu-err about 1 hour, the tongu about 15 minutes. Drain, reserving the tongu mushroom water. Discard the hard stems of the tongu mushrooms, then coarsely chop all the rest.

3 Heat 30 ml/2 tbsp of oil in a large frying pan (skillet) or wok. Stir-fry the mushrooms, bamboo shoots, soya bean sprouts, celery and carrots for 5 minutes.

4 Add 60 ml/4 tbsp of the mushroom water, the fish and oyster sauces, sprinkle with the sugar and cook for a further 2–3 minutes. Season with salt to taste. Keep warm.

5 Remove the chicken from the marinade, dab dry and lightly dust with flour. Shallow or deep-fry in hot oil for about 20 minutes until golden brown and cooked through.

6 Arrange the vegetables in bowls and place the chicken on top. Garnish each with a coriander leaf.

Chicken with Courgettes

GAENG KHUA FUK KAP KAI

PREPARATION TIME: 1½ HOURS
SERVES 4

SPICE PASTE:

1 large onion, finely chopped

1 head of garlic (12–14 cloves), peeled and crushed

15 ml/1 tbsp finely chopped lemon grass

5 ml/1 tsp grated galgant root (or 2.5 ml/½ tsp ground ginger

5 ml/1 tsp prawn (shrimp) paste (see page 25)

5 ml/1 tsp salt

5–10 ml/1–2 tsp sambal oelek (see page 25)

100 g/4 oz/1 cup creamed coconut

200 ml/7 fl oz/scant 1 cup water

4 chicken leg portions

salt

60 ml/4 tbsp oil

45 ml/3 tbsp tamarind juice (see page 23)

15 ml/1 tbsp palm or granulated sugar

30 ml/2 tbsp fish sauce (see page 24)

450 g/1 lb courgettes (zucchini), halved lengthways and sliced

To serve: Sambal oelek or Sharp Sauce (see pages 25, 28)

1 Pound all the spice paste ingredients in a pestle and mortar or in a bowl with the end of a rolling pin.

2 Mix the coconut with the water and melt slowly in a large frying pan (skillet) over a gentle heat.

3 Add the spice paste and simmer for about 5 minutes stirring occasionally.

4 Rub the chicken legs lightly with salt and then fry in the hot oil on both sides to brown. Place into the frying pan with the spiced coconut milk, cover and cook for 40 minutes, turning the chicken several times. 15 minutes before the end of the cooking time add the tamarind juice, the palm sugar and the fish sauce.

5 Add courgettes for the last 10 minutes of cooking time.

6 Taste and season, if necessary, with salt and serve with sambal oelek or Sharp Sauce.

COOK'S TIP: Use pumpkin instead of courgettes for a more authentic Thai flavour.

Thai Chicken Curry

GAENG PHED KAI

PREPARATION TIME: 30 MINUTES
SERVES 4

CHILLI PASTE:

5 dried chillies, crushed

10 garlic cloves, crushed

15 ml/1 tbsp grated galgant root (or 5 ml/1 tsp ground ginger)

5 ml/1 tsp grated lime or lemon rind

15 ml/1 tbsp finely chopped lemon grass

15 ml/1 tbsp ground coriander (cilantro)

Pinch of black pepper

15 ml/1 tbsp chopped coriander (cilantro)

5 ml/1 tsp salt

15 ml/1 tbsp prawn (shrimp) paste (see page 25)

30 ml/2 tbsp oil for frying

800 g/1¾ lb chicken breast cut in bite-sized pieces

200 ml/7 fl oz/scant 1 cup coconut milk (see page 18)

2 lime, lemon balm or mint leaves

45 ml/3 tbsp fish sauce (see page 24)

15 ml/1 tbsp palm or light brown sugar

225 g/8 oz/½ lb small whole makeur or aubergine (eggplant), diced

15 ml/1 tbsp chopped horapa or basil leaves

A few horapa or basil leaves to garnish

1 Pound all the chilli paste ingredients except oil in a pestle and mortar or in a bowl with the end of a rolling pin. Fry (sauté) in hot oil for 2 minutes, stirring.

2 Add the chicken and stir-fry for a further 3 minutes. Then add the coconut milk and gently simmer for about 10 minutes stirring occasionally.

3 Add the lime leaves, fish sauce and sugar and simmer gently for a further 5 minutes. Add the makeur and cook for 5 minutes. Discard lime leaves and stir in the chopped horapa leaves.

4 Serve garnished with a few whole horapa or basil leaves.

Chicken Curry with Tomatoes

GAENG PED KAI MAKEUA TAET

PREPARATION TIME: 1½ HOURS
SERVES 4

SPICE PASTE:

1 onion, finely chopped

4 garlic cloves, crushed

6-10 dried chillies, crushed

20 g/¾ oz/1½ tbsp lemon grass, finely chopped

15 ml/1 tbsp prawn (shrimp) paste (see page 25)

5 ml/1 tsp ground coriander (cilantro)

5 ml/1 tsp ground cross caraway or cumin

5 ml/1 tsp grated galgant root, or 2.5 ml/½ tsp ground ginger

2.5 ml/½ tsp white pepper

65 g/2½ oz/good ½ cup creamed coconut (Santen; see page 18)

Salt

4 chicken leg portions

400 ml/14 fl oz/1¾ cups coconut milk (see page 18)

15-30 ml/1-2 tbsp fish sauce (see page 24)

15-30 ml/1-2 tbsp tamarind juice (see page 23)

15 ml/1 tbsp sugar

4-6 tomatoes, quartered

Sprigs of coriander (cilantro) to garnish

1 Pound all ingredients for the spice paste together in a pestle and mortar or in a bowl with the end of a rolling pin.

2 Slowly melt the creamed coconut in a large frying pan (skillet) then add the spice paste and stir fry for 2 to 3 minutes.

3 Rub a little salt into the chicken, place in the pan and coat with the coconut spice mixture. Pour on the coconut milk and season with fish sauce, tamarind juice and sugar. Cover and cook over a moderate heat for a further 30-40 minutes until chicken is tender, turning several times.

4 Reserve a few tomato wedges for garnish, add remainder to the pan. Turn up the heat and cook quickly for a further 3 to 4 minutes. Serve garnished with the reserved tomatoes and sprigs of coriander.

Chicken Ragout with Spices

KAI TUNG

PREPARATION TIME: 1 HOUR
SERVES 4-6

CHILLI PASTE:

6 dried chillies, crushed

4 shallots or 1-2 onions, finely chopped

6 garlic cloves, crushed

1-2 small pieces lemon grass, finely chopped

5 ml/1 tsp ground ginger

1-2 small pieces fresh galgant root, grated or an extra 2.5 ml/½ tsp ground ginger

5 ml/1 tsp ground coriander

2.5 ml/½ tsp cinnamon

5 ml/1 tsp each salt and pepper

75-90 ml/5-6 tbsp oil for frying

1 poularde or large roasting chicken, about 1.75 kg/4 lb, cut in 4-6 pieces

400 ml/14 fl oz/1¾ cups chicken stock (see page 26)

30-45 ml/2-3 tbsp fish sauce (see page 24)

30-45 ml/2-3 tbsp tamarind juice (see page 23)

Coriander (cilantro) leaves to garnish

1 Pound all the spice paste ingredients except the oil in a pestle and mortar or in a bowl with the end of a rolling pin.

2 Heat the oil in a large frying pan (skillet) or wok and fry (sauté) the paste stirring for 1-2 minutes.

3 Add the chicken pieces and turn until completely coated in the spice paste.

4 Add the chicken stock, bring to the boil, reduce heat, cover and simmer for 45 minutes until meat is tender.

5 Should the sauce not have reduced, boil rapidly, uncovered for up to 10 minutes.

6 Season with the fish sauce, tamarind juice and add salt if necessary. Serve garnished with coriander.

Siamese Chicken Breast

KAI TORD

PREPARATION TIME: 20 MINUTES
PLUS MARINATING TIME
SERVES 4

---

10 garlic cloves, crushed

15 ml/1 tbsp white pepper

5–10 ml/1–2 tsp ground
coriander (cilantro)

5 ml/1 tsp salt

4 large chicken breasts

60 ml/4 tbsp oil for frying

To serve: Sharp Sauce and
Sweet Fish Sauce
(see pages 28 and 29)

1 Pound the garlic with the
pepper, the coriander and the
salt in a pestle and mortar or in a
bowl with the end of a rolling pin
to a fine paste. Rub it into the
chicken breasts and leave to stand
for 30 minutes.

2 Heat oil until very hot in a
large pan and fry (sauté) the
chicken quickly to brown.

3 Reduce the heat and fry the
meat gently, turning often
until cooked through. Serve with
the sauces.

Fried Duck with Pineapple

GAENG PED SUPPAROT

PREPARATION TIME: 2 HOURS
SERVES 2–3

1 oven-ready duck (about 2 kg/ 4½ lb)

600 ml/1 pt/2½ cups water

75 g/3 oz/¾ cup creamed coconut (Santen; see page 18)

30–45 ml/2–3 tbsp red spice paste (see page 34)

200 g/7 oz/1¾ cups diced fresh (or drained canned) pineapple

200 g/7 oz/1¾ cups drained, canned bamboo shoots

30–45 ml/2–3 tbsp fish sauce (see page 24)

15 ml/1 tbsp sugar

Juice of ½ lemon

45 ml/3 tbsp chopped horapa or basil

1 Preheat the oven to 240°C/ 475°F/gas mark 9. Cut the duck into 6 pieces. Remove fat.

2 Place the duck pieces in a roasting tin (pan) and add 250 ml/8 fl oz/1 cup of the water. Cook in the oven for about 45 minutes, turn from time to time. Then pour off the fat and remove the skin from the duck pieces.

3 Place the creamed coconut with the remaining water in a pan and melt over a gentle heat. Stir in the spice paste. Add the duck, cover and simmer for 45 minutes. Turn often.

4 Add the pineapple and bamboo shoots together with the fish sauce, sugar, and lemon juice 15 minutes before the end of the cooking. Sprinkle the herbs over just before serving.

Green Duck Curry

GAENG KEO WAN PET

PREPARATION TIME: 2 HOURS
SERVES 4

1 oven-ready duck
(about 2.25 kg/5 lb)

45 ml/3 tbsp oil

75 ml/5 tbsp green spice paste
(see page 35)

1 litre/1¾ pts/4¼ cups coconut
milk (see page 18)

Salt

8 lemon, lemon balm or mint
leaves

25 g/1 oz/2 tbsp lemon grass,
finely chopped

30 ml/2 tbsp fish sauce (see
page 24)

3 green (bell) peppers, seeded
and cut in diamond shapes

8-10 horapa or basil leaves

1 Remove all visible fat from the duck and cut the bird into 6-8 pieces.

2 Heat the oil in a large frying pan (skillet) and quickly fry (sauté) the duck pieces on all sides to brown.

3 Add the green spice paste, and stir-fry for a further 2-3 minutes.

4 Add the coconut milk, a little salt and the lemon leaves, lemon grass and fish sauce. Half cover and simmer for 45-60 minutes until the duck meat is very tender and the coconut milk has reduced a little.

5 Add the green pepper pieces and cook uncovered for a further 4-5 minutes. Should the sauce become too thick, add some coconut milk or water.

6 Remove the pan from the heat and leave to stand for a while, then spoon off the fat.

7 Re-heat, taste and if necessary season again with fish sauce and sprinkle with horapa leaves before serving.

Chicken Liver with Mushrooms

TAB KAI KAB HED

PREPARATION TIME: 30 MINUTES
PLUS SOAKING TIME
SERVES 3–4

---

6 dried mu-err (Chinese cloud ear) mushrooms

6 dried tongu (shiitake) mushrooms

10 ml/2 tsp sugar

30 ml/2 tbsp vinegar

60 ml/4 tbsp oil

2 onions, halved and sliced

50 g/2 oz/½ cup fresh root ginger, grated

1 bunch of spring onions (scallions), sliced

100 g/4 oz/1 cup sliced leek

1 large onion, chopped

4 fresh red chillies, seeded and cut in thin rings

1 small red (bell) pepper, diced

1 small green (bell) pepper, diced

450 g/1 lb/4 cups chicken livers, cut in bite-sized pieces

30–45 ml/2–3 tbsp fish sauce (see page 24)

Salt

1 Soak the different mushrooms separately in lukewarm water: the mu-err mushrooms for about 1 hour, the tongu mushrooms for about 15 minutes. Drain, reserving the water from the tongu mushrooms. Cut out the hard stalks of the tongu mushrooms and discard. Cut all the mushrooms into strips.

2 Mix the sugar and the vinegar together and place on one side.

3 Heat the oil in a large frying pan (skillet) and fry (sauté) the onions until golden brown. Add the ginger, spring onions, leek, chillies, mushrooms and the peppers and stir-fry for 3–4 minutes.

4 Add the pieces of liver and stir-fry for 1 minute, then add the sugar and vinegar mixture along with 45–60 ml/3–4 tbsp of the soaking water from the tongu mushrooms and cook for 4–5 minutes. Season with the fish sauce and add salt to taste.

Seafood Dishes

*Sometimes exotic, sometimes simple,
always colourful and exciting – Thai fish
cookery is among the best in the world.
The cooking times are always short,
retaining all the taste and
goodness of the catch.
Never be afraid to experiment with
different fish from those suggested.
And always serve plain boiled rice as an
accompaniment.*

Fried Hake with Mango Sauce

MUANG LI

PREPARATION TIME: 45 MINUTES
SERVES 4–6

SAUCE:

2 unripe green mangoes, peeled, stoned (pitted) and chopped

1 small onion, finely chopped

2 fresh red chillies, seeded and cut into thin rings

60 ml/4 tbsp fish sauce (see page 24)

30–45 ml/2–3 tbsp sugar

4 dried prawns (shrimps) or 30–45 ml/2–3 tbsp prawn (shrimp) paste (see page 25)

100 g/4 oz/1 cup desiccated (shredded) coconut

40 g/1½ oz/⅓ cup cashew nuts

3–4 small dried chillies, crushed

4–6 hake steaks (about 800 g/ 1¾ lb in all)

75 g/3 oz/¾ cup plain (all-purpose) flour

5 ml/1 tsp each of salt and pepper

Oil for frying

Lettuce leaves, tomatoes, cucumber for garnish

1 To make the sauce mix the mango, the onion and the chillies together with the fish sauce, sugar and the dried prawns or prawn paste.

2 Dry-fry the coconut in a frying pan (skillet) until golden brown and mix with the mango sauce. Toast the cashew nuts in the same way and then sprinkle with the crushed dried chillies.

3 Rinse the hake and dab dry well.

4 Mix the flour, salt and pepper and mix with a little cold water to a sticky batter. Brush all over the fish.

5 Pour enough oil into a frying pan or a fish fryer, so that it is 1 cm/½ in deep. Fry the fish, turning over, for 10–12 minutes until it is crisp, golden and cooked through. Drain on kitchen paper.

6 Cut the tomatoes into eighths, peel the cucumber and cut into not too thin slices. Arrange the lettuce leaves on a serving plate, place the fried fish on top, and decorate with slices of cucumber and pieces of tomato. Serve the sauce separately.

Steamed Sea Bass in Soy Sauce

PLA KAPHONG KAO NEUNG SI LU

PREPARATION TIME: 40 MINUTES
SERVES 3-4

5 dried tongu (shiitake) mushrooms

1 cleaned and scaled sea bass (about 800 g/1¾ lb)

100 ml/3½ fl oz/6½ tbsp soy sauce

15 ml/1 tbsp sugar

1 rasher (slice) fat, smoked bacon, diced

2-3 spring onions (scallions), sliced

1 Leave the tongu mushrooms to soak in lukewarm water for about 15 minutes. Drain, reserving the water. Remove tough stalks, then slice the caps.

2 Place the fish in a fish kettle or roasting tin (pan) large enough to hold it flat.

3 Mix the soy sauce with the sugar and mushroom water. Pour over the fish, and arrange the bacon, spring onions and the mushrooms over. Cover with a lid or foil and cook the fish for about 20 minutes over a gentle heat, turning once and adding a little water if necessary.

Thai Fish Croquettes

PLA SAWAN THOT

PREPARATION TIME: 40 MINUTES
SERVES 3-4

1 onion, finely chopped

4 garlic cloves, crushed

450 g/1 lb white fish fillet (cod, hake etc), skinned

5 ml/1 tsp salt

5 ml/1 tsp white pepper

1 egg, beaten

45-60 ml/3-4 tbsp plain (all-purpose) flour

50 g/2 oz/1 cup fresh breadcrumbs

oil for frying

SAUCE:

60 ml/4 tbsp red wine vinegar

15-30 ml/1-2 tbsp sugar

2.5 ml/½ tsp salt

Cayenne to taste

Twists of lime or lemon to garnish

1 Purée or finely mince (grind) the onion, garlic and fish in a food processor or mincer (grinder).

2 Place the fish mixture in a bowl, add salt, pepper, egg and sufficient flour to bind.

3 Shape into small rissoles or fingers about 10 cm/4 in long, roll in the breadcrumbs and fry (sauté) in plenty of hot oil on both sides until crispy brown. Drain on kitchen paper.

4 Mix the vinegar with sugar, salt and cayenne to taste. Arrange the fried fish croquettes on a serving plate. Garnish with twists of lime or lemon and serve the sauce separately.

Fried Hake with Onion and Chilli Sauce

PLA KAO RAT PRIK

PREPARATION TIME: 40 MINUTES
SERVES 2-3

2-3 onions, finely chopped

8 garlic cloves, crushed

4-5 dried chillies, crushed

60 ml/4 tbsp oil

15-30 ml/1-2 tbsp chopped coriander (cilantro)

45 ml/3 tbsp tamarind juice (see page 23)

15 ml/1 tbsp palm or granulated sugar

30-45 ml/2-3 tbsp fish sauce (see page 24)

Salt

450 g/1 lb hake fillet, skinned

Oil for frying

Lemon or lime slices and coriander (cilantro) sprigs to garnish

COOK'S TIP: This sauce goes well with any other kind of fried fish fillet.

1 Fry (sauté) the onions, garlic and chillies in 45 ml/3 tbsp of the oil, without browning.

2 Add the coriander, tamarind juice, sugar and fish sauce, stir and season with salt if necessary.

3 Fry (sauté) the hake in remaining oil for about 10 minutes, turning once until cooked through.

4 Arrange the hake on a plate, garnish with lemon or lime slices and a sprig of coriander and serve the sauce separately.

Butterfish with Mushrooms

PLA JALAMET KHAO
NEUNG KIAM BUAI

PREPARATION TIME: 1 HOUR
SERVES 3-4

6 dried tongu (shiitake) mushrooms

1 cleaned butterfish or sea bream (about 1 kg/2¼ lb)

Oil for greasing

2-3 Chinese preserved plums, chopped or 15 ml/1 tbsp plum or hoisin sauce

100 g/4 oz/¼ lb piece smoked fat bacon, diced

2.5 cm/1 in piece fresh root ginger, grated

100 g/4 oz/1 cup chopped celery

30 ml/2 tbsp fish sauce (see page 24)

2.5 ml/½ tsp cayenne

1 Leave the mushrooms to soak in lukewarm water for 15 minutes. Drain, reserving the water. Remove tough stalks, then slice the caps.

2 Using a sharp knife make slashes on both sides of the fish. Brush an ovenproof dish with oil and place the fish in it.

3 Mix the mushrooms, plums, bacon, ginger and celery together with the fish sauce, cayenne and 45 ml/3 tbsp of the mushroom liquid and spread over the fish.

4 Cover the dish with foil and place in a steamer or in a roasting tin (pan) of hot water and cook the fish for 15-20 minutes. Carefully transfer to a serving plate and serve hot.

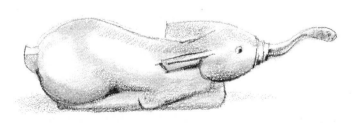

Fried Fish Fillets with Ginger

PLA CHIEN

PREPARATION TIME: 30 MINUTES
SERVES 4

800g/1¾ lb fish fillets (hake, cod or sole)

Salt

150 ml/¼ pt/⅔ cup oil

50 g/2 oz/½ cup fresh root ginger, grated

6 garlic cloves, crushed

30 ml/2 tbsp palm or soft brown sugar

45 ml/3 tbsp fish sauce (see page 24)

60 ml/4 tbsp tamarind juice (see page 23)

2 onions, finely chopped

Coriander (cilantro) leaves to garnish

1 Rub the fish fillets with some salt. Heat the oil in a large frying pan (skillet) and fry (sauté) the fillets on both sides until golden brown. Drain on kitchen paper. Pour all but 45 ml/3 tbsp of the hot oil out of the pan and reserve.

2 Stir-fry the ginger in the remaining oil over a moderate heat for 1 minute, then add the garlic and fry for a further 1 minute.

3 Add the sugar, fish sauce and tamarind juice, simmer gently until the sugar has dissolved. Add a little water if necessary. Return fish to the sauce to heat through.

4 Fry (sauté) the onion in a fresh pan in a little of the reserved oil until golden. Remove with a draining spoon.

5 Arrange the fish fillets on warm serving plates, pour on the sauce and sprinkle with the fried onions and coriander leaves to garnish.

Steamed Sea Bream

PLA KUTSALAT NEUNG SI LU

PREPARATION TIME: 25 MINUTES
SERVES 2–3

1 cleaned and scaled sea bream
(800 g/1¾ lb)

2 cm/¾ in piece fresh root
ginger, grated

2 dried chillies, grated

3 spring onions (scallions),
sliced

30 ml/2 tbsp oyster sauce

30 ml/2 tbsp soy sauce

5 ml/1 tsp sugar

2.5 ml/½ tsp white pepper

2.5 ml/½ tsp ground coriander
(cilantro)

Salt to taste

1 Place the bream on a heat
resistant plate.

2 Place the plate in a steamer
and steam the fish for about 8
minutes.

3 Mix remaining ingredients
together and pour over fish.
Steam for a further 5–8 minutes or
until fish is just cooked through.
Serve hot.

*COOK'S TIP: The fish can be
wrapped in a piece of foil with the
other ingredients and placed in the
oven in a water bath (a deep pan
filled with hot water) and baked at
230°C/450°F/gas mark 8 for about
15–20 minutes.*

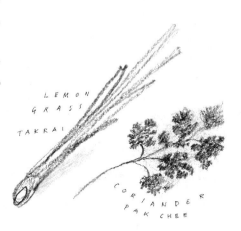

LEMON
GRASS
TAKRAI

CORIANDER
PAK CHEE

Fried Tuna Fish with Soy Sauce

PLA O YANG SI LU

PREPARATION TIME: 20 MINUTES
SERVES 2

2 tuna steaks (about 225g/8 oz/ ½ lb each)

100 ml/3½ fl oz/6½ tbsp oil

45–60 ml/3–4 tbsp soy sauce

¼ cucumber, strips of skin removed then sliced

3 tomatoes, sliced

2 spring onions, (scallions), finely chopped

Coriander (cilantro) leaves to garnish

1 Fry (sauté) the fish in the oil on both sides until crispy brown and cooked through. Drain on kitchen paper then transfer to warm plates.

2 Sprinkle with the soy sauce. Lay the cucumber and tomato slices attractively to one side and sprinkle fish with the spring onions and a few coriander leaves.

COOK'S TIP: Any fish fillets are delicious cooked in this way.

Smoke-Cooked Sea Pike

PLA SAMLI ROM KHWAN

PREPARATION TIME: 40 MINUTES
SERVES 2

1 large or 2 small cleaned sea pike (garfish or baracuda)

5 ml/1 tsp ground turmeric

15 ml/1 tbsp oil

10 ml/2 tsp rice or white wine vinegar

Salt and pepper

2.5 ml/½ tsp ground ginger

SAUCE:

3–4 fresh red chillies, seeded and finely chopped

3–4 garlic cloves, crushed

45 ml/3 tbsp lime or lemon juice

45 ml/3 tbsp tamarind juice (see page 23)

5 ml/1 tsp sugar

1 Lay the fish in a shallow metal roasting tin (pan).

2 Mix the turmeric with the oil, the vinegar and the ginger and season with salt and pepper. Brush all over fish and leave for 2 hours.

3 Place the roasting tin on a hot, smokey barbecue and cook the fish, turning once.

4 Mix sauce ingredients together and serve separately.

COOK'S TIP: Originally the fish were smoked plain in a smoking oven then served with the sauce. But this barbecued version is much more practical for most people and is a delicious way of serving mackerel or herring too.

Hake with Cashew Dressing

PLA KAO PHAT HAENG

PREPARATION TIME: 30 MINUTES
SERVES 4

3 dried tongu (shiitake) mushrooms

3 small carrots, sliced and cut in attractive shapes, if liked

1 onion, chopped

60 ml/4 tbsp oil

100 g/4 oz/1 cup diced boiled ham

4-6 baby sweetcorn cobs

40 g/1½ oz/⅓ cup cashew nuts

45 ml/3 tbsp soy sauce

2.5 ml/½ tsp white pepper

Salt

800 g/1¾ lb hake fillets

Flour for dusting

1 Leave the mushrooms to soak in lukewarm water for about 15 minutes. Drain, reserving the soaking water. Discard the tough stalks and cut the caps into strips.

2 Fry (sauté) the carrot and onion in 30 ml/2 tbsp of the oil for 2 minutes, stirring.

3 Add the mushrooms, ham, sweetcorn cobs, soy sauce and 45 ml/3 tbsp of the mushroom soaking water. Simmer uncovered for 5 minutes.

4 Add the cashew nuts, mix with the vegetables and season with pepper and salt.

5 Meanwhile toss the fish fillets in seasoned flour and fry (sauté) in remaining oil until crispy and golden brown on both sides and cooked through.

6 Arrange the fish fillets on serving plates and spoon over the sauce.

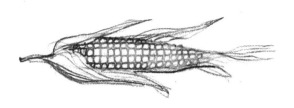

Sea Pike with Mango

PLA SAMLI SONG KHRENANG

PREPARATION TIME: 30 MINUTES
SERVES 4

SAUCE:

1 unripe mango, peeled, stoned (pitted) and chopped

1 small onion, finely chopped

2.5 ml/½ tsp salt

5 ml/1 tsp dried prawns (shrimp) (or prawn (shrimp) paste see page 25)

2.5 ml/½ tsp sugar

2.5 ml/½ tsp cayenne

800 g/1¾ lb sea pike (garfish or baracuda) fillets

45 ml/3 tbsp fish sauce (see page 24)

Flour for dusting

60 ml/4 tbsp oil

Lettuce leaves to garnish

1 Mix sauce ingredients together and turn into a little dish.

2 Brush the fish fillets all over with fish sauce and dust with flour.

3 Heat the oil in a frying pan (skillet) and fry (sauté) the fillets on both sides until crispy brown and cooked through.

4 Place the lettuce leaves on plates and arrange the fish fillets on them. Serve the sauce separately.

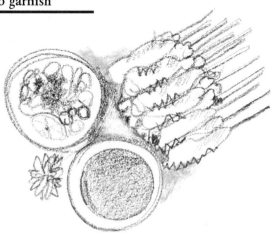

Crabs with Egg and Chilli Sauce

PU PHAT PHRIK

PREPARATION TIME: 1 HOUR
SERVES 2-4

2 live edible crabs (each about 800 g/1¾ lb)

Salt

4 dried tongu (shiitake) mushrooms

4 garlic cloves, crushed

200 g/7 oz/1¾ cups drained, canned bamboo shoots, cut in strips

50 g/2 oz/½ cup sliced celery

30 ml/2 tbsp oil

75 ml/5 tbsp fish or chicken stock (see pages 26 and 27)

30 ml/2 tbsp soy sauce

15 ml/1 tbsp tomato ketchup (catsup)

15 ml/1 tbsp oyster sauce

3 fresh red chillies, seeded and cut in thin rings

45 ml/3 tbsp medium hot chilli sauce

15 ml/1 tbsp sugar

2 eggs

60 ml/4 tbsp milk

COOK'S TIP: If you prefer, buy freshly cooked crab.

1 Place the edible crabs head first into boiling, lightly salted water and cook for 5 minutes in a covered saucepan. Leave the crabs to cool a little in the water and then remove.

2 Soak the tongu mushrooms in lukewarm water for about 15 minutes. Drain, remove the tough stalks and cut the caps into thin strips.

3 Divide the crabs using a knife, remove the meat, including that from the claws and legs. Also remove the edible parts of the stomach. Place the meat on one side. Reserve claws for garnish.

4 In a frying pan (skillet), fry (sauté) the mushrooms, garlic, bamboo and celery in the oil for 2 minutes, stirring. Add the fish or chicken stock, the soy sauce, ketchup and oyster sauce. Simmer for 1 minute.

5 Add the chillies, chilli sauce, sugar and the crab meat and heat through.

6 Whisk the eggs with the milk, lightly salt, pour into the frying pan stir occasionally until it sets. Spoon on to plates and garnish with the crab claws.

Crabs in Tamarind Juice with Vegetables

GAENG SOM PU

PREPARATION TIME: 40 MINUTES
SERVES 2-4

2 live crabs (about 800 g/1¾ lb each)

Salt

CHILLI PASTE:

5 small dried chillies, crushed

6 garlic cloves, crushed

4 shallots or 1 small onion, finely chopped

15 ml/1 tbsp prawn (shrimp) paste (see page 25)

500 ml/17 fl oz/2¼ cups water

100 g/4 oz/1 cup thin green beans, cut in thirds

50 g/2 oz/½ cup Chinese sour preserved vegetables (obtainable in Asian and other specialist food shops), cut in thin strips

100 g/4 oz/1 cup canned, drained bamboo shoots, cut in thin strips

150 g/5 oz/1¼ cups shredded Chinese leaves (stem lettuce)

30-45 ml/2-3 tbsp fish sauce (see page 24)

60 ml/4 tbsp tamarind juice (see page 23)

1 Place the crabs head first into boiling lightly salted water, cover and cook for 5 minutes, then remove and leave to cool.

2 Mix Chilli paste ingredients together with 2.5 ml/½ tsp salt in a saucepan.

3 Add the water and bring to the boil.

4 Add the beans and simmer for 10 minutes. Add remaining vegetables and simmer for a further 5 minutes.

5 Meanwhile, break open the crabs with a knife and remove the meat, including that from the claws and legs. Reserve the claws for garnish. Cut the shell down the centre and remove the edible parts. Add the crab meat to the saucepan.

6 Heat through, season with fish sauce and tamarind juice and serve garnished with the crab claws.

King Prawns with Broccoli

PHAD KUNG

PREPARATION TIME: 25 MINUTES
SERVES 4

450 g/1 lb broccoli, divided
into florets and stalks cut in
small pieces

Salt

16–20 king prawns (jumbo
shrimp) with shells

4 garlic cloves, crushed

60 ml/4 tbsp oil

15 ml/1 tbsp soy sauce

15 ml/1 tbsp oyster sauce

1 First cook the broccoli stalks in boiling, salted water for about 5 minutes, then add the florets and cook for a further 5 minutes. Drain well.

2 Peel the king prawns and remove the black thread down each back.

3 Heat 30 ml/2 tbsp of the oil in a large frying pan (skillet) and fry (sauté) the king prawns on both sides for 1–2 minutes stirring all the time.

4 Add the broccoli and garlic and stir fry for another 30 seconds. Season the dish with soy and oyster sauces and serve immediately.

King Prawns with Salted Beans

KUNG AWENG

PREPARATION TIME: 15 MINUTES
SERVES 2-3

800 g/1¾ lb king prawns (jumbo shrimp) with shells

60 ml/4 tbsp oil

15 ml/1 tbsp salted beans (from Asian and other specialist food shops)

30 ml/2 tbsp oyster sauce

15 ml/1 tbsp sugar

15–30 ml/1–2 tbsp dry sherry

15 ml/1 tbsp sesame oil

1 Peel the king prawns but leave on the tail fins. Remove the black thread down each back.

2 Heat half the oil in a frying pan (skillet) and fry (sauté) the king prawns in it for about 2 minutes on each side until golden brown.

3 Heat remaining oil in a separate pan and fry the salted beans in it for 2–3 minutes. Add the oyster sauce, sugar, sherry and the sesame oil and stir-fry for 2 minutes.

4 Place the king prawns in the sauce and turn until completely covered in the sauce. Serve hot.

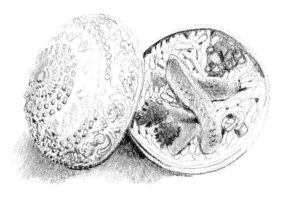

Steamed King Prawns with Soy Sauce

KUNG KULA DAM NEUNG SI LU

PREPARATION TIME: 15 MINUTES
SERVES 2

12 king prawns (jumbo shrimp) with shells

2 garlic cloves, crushed

30 ml/2 tbsp chopped coriander (cilantro)

30 ml/2 tbsp oyster sauce

45 ml/3 tbsp soy sauce

Pinch of white pepper

2 spring onions (scallions), sliced

1 Peel the king prawns and remove the black thread down each back. Arrange on a heat resistant plate.

2 Mix the garlic with the coriander, the oyster and soy sauces and the pepper. Pour over the king prawns, place the plate in a steamer and steam for 10 minutes. Or, wrap the plate in foil, stand in a roasting tin (pan) of hot water and bake at 200°C/400°F/ gas mark 6 for about the same amount of time.

3 Sprinkle the spring onion over before serving.

Raw King Prawns with Fish Sauce

KUNG CHAE NAM PLA

**PREPARATION TIME: 15 MINUTES
PLUS CHILLING TIME
SERVES 2**

10–12 very fresh king prawns (jumbo shrimp) with shells

6 garlic cloves, peeled

2–6 fresh red chillies, seeded and sliced into thin rings

30 ml/2 tbsp chopped coriander (cilantro)

30 ml/2 tbsp fish sauce (see page 24)

30 ml/2 tbsp lime or lemon juice

5 ml/1 tsp sugar

Salt

15 ml/1 tbsp chopped mint

1 Peel the king prawns but leave on the tail fins. Remove the black thread down the back of each. Arrange the king prawns on a plate in a circle. Chill.

2 Place four of the whole garlic cloves between the king prawns.

3 Crush the remainder and mix with the remaining ingredients. Chill.

4 Pour the sauce over the king prawns just before serving.

King Prawns with Palm Hearts

KUNG PHAT KHI MAO YOT MAPHRAO ON

PREPARATION TIME: 20 MINUTES
SERVES 2

10-12 peeled king prawns (jumbo shrimp)

6 garlic cloves, crushed

2-6 fresh red chillies, seeded and chopped

2.5 ml/½ tsp ground coriander (cilantro)

45 ml/3 tbsp oil

250 g/9 oz/2¼ cups drained, canned palm hearts, cut in 1 cm/½ in pieces

15 ml/1 tbsp fish sauce (see page 24)

15 ml/1 tbsp oyster sauce

5 ml/1 tsp sugar

Salt

100 ml/3½ fl oz/6½ tbsp fish stock (see page 27)

A few horapa or coriander (cilantro) leaves for garnish

1 Remove the black thread down the back of each prawn.

2 Pound the garlic, chillies and coriander in a pestle and mortar or in a bowl with the end of a rolling pin. Stir-fry in the hot oil for 1 minute.

3 Add the king prawns and turn in the spice mixture.

4 Add the palm hearts and heat through.

5 Stir in the fish sauce and oyster sauce, sugar, salt and fish stock and simmer for 1 to 2 minutes. Sprinkle with horapa or coriander leaves to garnish before serving.

Sweet and Sour Seafood

THALE SUAN KAEO

PREPARATION TIME: 45 MINUTES
SERVES 4

200 g/7 oz/scant ½ lb king prawns (jumbo shrimp) with shells

450 g/1 lb fresh scrubbed mussels, beards removed

450 g/1 lb white fish fillet

200 g/7 oz/scant ½ lb squid, cleaned

Salt

30 ml/2 tbsp butter

30–45 ml/2–3 tbsp plain (all-purpose) flour

300 ml/½ pt/1¼ cups fish stock (see page 27)

5 ml/1 tsp white pepper

5–10 ml/1–2 tsp sugar

15 ml/1 tbsp fish sauce (see page 24)

45 ml/3 tbsp tomato ketchup (catsup)

1 green (bell) pepper, seeded and diced

3 tomatoes, seeded and cut in wedges

150 g/5 oz/1¼ cups fresh or drained canned diced pineapple

2 onions, sliced

15 ml/1 tbsp oil

1 Peel the king prawns, leaving on the tail fins and remove the black thread down each back.

2 Discard any damaged or open mussels.

3 Cut the fish fillet into large cubes, the squid into strips. Cook seafood one type at a time in a little salted water (squid 15 minutes, mussels 10 minutes, fish 5 minutes, prawns 2 minutes). The mussels should be open, discard closed ones.

4 Melt the butter in a large saucepan, stir in the flour and cook 1 minute. Stir in the fish stock and season with salt, the pepper, sugar, fish sauce and the ketchup.

5 Add the green (bell) pepper, the tomatoes and the pineapple, and simmer for 5 minutes.

6 Remove the mussels from the shells and add with the prawns, squid and fish to the sauce. Should this be too thick, add a little of the fish cooking water. Heat through for 2 to 3 minutes.

7 Meanwhile, fry (sauté) the onion slices in the oil until crisp and golden and sprinkle over.

Fried Squid Rings

PLA MEUK THOT

PREPARATION TIME: 40 MINUTES
SERVES 4

6 garlic cloves, crushed

2.5 ml/½ tsp salt

2.5 ml/½ tsp pepper

60-75 ml/4-5 tbsp soy sauce

800 g/1¾ lb cleaned squid rings (fresh or thawed, frozen)

Tapioca, rice or plain (all-purpose) flour for dusting

Oil for deep frying

SAUCE:

100 ml/3½ fl oz/6½ tbsp red wine vinegar

30-45 ml/2-3 tbsp sugar

2.5 ml/½ tsp cayenne

1 Mix the garlic with the salt, pepper and soy sauce. Turn the squid rings in it and marinate for 30 minutes.

2 Heat oil for deep frying to 190°C/375°F (or until a cube of day-old bread browns in 30 seconds). Dust the squid rings with flour.

3 Bring the vinegar to the boil in a small saucepan, add sugar, 5 ml/1 tsp salt and the cayenne and simmer, stirring until the sugar has dissolved.

4 Deep-fry the squid rings in the hot oil until golden brown. Drain on kitchen paper and serve hot with the sauce.

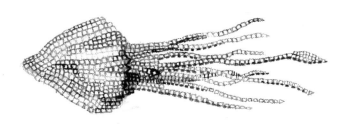

Seafood in Tamarind Juice

KAENG SOM RUAM MIT THALE

PREPARATION TIME: 1 HOUR
SERVES 2–3

5 fresh red chillies, seeded and sliced into thin rings

6 shallots or 3 onions, finely chopped

10 garlic cloves, crushed

5 ml/1 tsp prawn (shrimp) paste (see page 25)

2.5 ml/½ tsp salt

2.5 ml/½ tsp sugar

100 ml/3½ fl oz/6½ tbsp tamarind juice (see page 23)

500 ml/17 fl oz/2¼ cups water

100 g/4 oz/1 cup sliced green beans

100 g/4 oz/1 cup sliced carrots, cut in attractive shapes if liked

100 g/4 oz/1 cup shredded Chinese leaves (stem lettuce)

6 king prawns (jumbo shrimp) with shells

Meat from 1 boiled crab or 200g/7 oz/scant 1 cup canned crab meat

200 g/7 oz/scant 1 cup squid, cut in rings

300 g/11 oz/scant ¾ lb cooked cockles (drained if in brine)

200 g/7 oz/scant ½ lb red mullet fillet, cut in bite-sized pieces

To serve: Sharp Sauce (see page 28)

1 Mix the chillies with the shallots, garlic, prawn paste, salt, sugar and tamarind juice in a saucepan. Add the water and bring to the boil.

2 Add the beans and carrots. Boil for about 10 minutes until just cooked. Add the Chinese leaves and cook for 1 minute.

3 Peel the king prawns, leaving on the tail fins. Remove the black thread down each back.

4 Add all the seafood except the crab to the simmering stock and cook very gently for 5–10 minutes.

5 Add the crab meat, heat through and serve piping hot with a bowl of Sharp Sauce.

Baked Oysters with Salted Beans

HOI NANG ROM OP TAO SI

PREPARATION TIME: 10 MINUTES
SERVES 2

12 fresh oysters

15 ml/1 tbsp pork dripping

60 ml/4 tbsp salted black beans (from Asian and other specialist food shops)

6 garlic cloves, halved

2 cm/¾ in piece fresh root ginger, grated

30–45 ml/2–3 tbsp chopped coriander (cilantro)

1 Scrub the oysters. Then take each one in a cloth with the curved side downwards in the hand, then using an oyster knife cut into the hinge and separate it.

2 Lift off the upper shell. Place the shell containing the oysters on a heat resistant flat plate.

3 Preheat the oven to 230°C/450°F/gas mark 8. Heat the dripping in a small saucepan and stir-fry the beans for 1–2 minutes.

4 Add the ginger then spread this mixture over the oysters.

5 Place half a garlic clove on each oyster. Bake in the oven for about 5 minutes.

6 Sprinkle with coriander and serve.

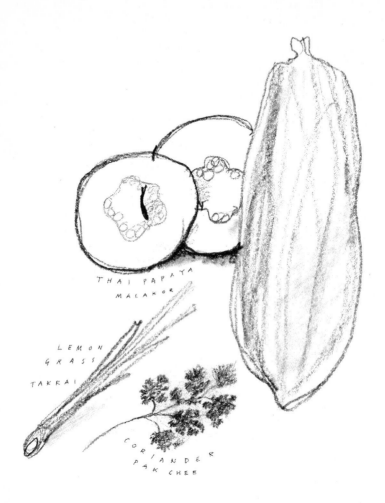

THAI PAPAYA
MALAKOR

LEMON
GRASS
TAKRAI

CORIANDER
PAK CHEE

Rice and Noodle Dishes

*All these dishes can be made from
leftovers of meat, fish or vegetables.
Served with a side dish or salad they
make colourful, filling and nutritious
value-for-money meals.*

Vegetable Rice

KAO PAT TAMADA

PREPARATION TIME: 45 MINUTES
PLUS SOAKING TIME
SERVES 4

3 mu-err (Chinese cloud ear) mushrooms

3 dried tongu (shiitake) mushrooms

350 g/12 oz/1½ cups long-grain rice

45–60 ml/3–4 tbsp oil

2 onions, finely chopped

5–6 garlic cloves, crushed

2.5 cm/½ in piece fresh root ginger, grated

1 red (bell) pepper, seeded and diced

1 green (bell) pepper, seeded and diced

200 g/7 oz/1¾ cups chopped celery

150 g/5 oz/1¼ cups soya bean sprouts

150 g/5 oz/1¼ cups drained, canned bamboo shoots cut in strips

45 ml/3 tbsp soy sauce

30 ml/2 tbsp fish sauce (see page 24)

Coriander (cilantro) leaves to garnish

1 Soak the mu-err mushrooms in lukewarm water for about 1 hour. Drain, rinse with cold water, drain again and cut into thin strips. Soak the tongu mushrooms in lukewarm water for about 15 minutes. Discard tough stalks and cut caps into thin strips.

2 Boil the rice in plenty of boiling salted water until tender, about 15 minutes. Drain, rinse with boiling water and drain again.

3 Heat the oil in a frying pan (skillet) and fry (sauté) the onions until golden. Add the garlic and ginger and stir-fry for 1 minute.

4 Add the mushrooms, peppers, celery, bean sprouts and bamboo shoots and stir-fry for 5 minutes.

5 Mix in the rice and season the dish with soy and fish sauce. Sprinkle with coriander leaves before serving.

Rice in Coconut Milk

KAO MAN

PREPARATION TIME: 25 MINUTES
SERVES 4 AS AN ACCOMPANIMENT

300 g/11 oz/1⅓ cups long-grain rice

Scant 600 ml/1 pt/2½ cups coconut milk (see page 18)

5–10 ml/1–2 tsp salt

15 ml/1 tbsp sugar

To serve: Papaya Salad (see page 54) or any meat or fish dish

1 Rinse the rice thoroughly under running water and leave to drain.

2 Put in a saucepan with the coconut milk, add the salt and sugar and boil rapidly for 10–15 minutes uncovered.

3 Cover the saucepan and let the rice swell over the gentlest heat. Serve with Papaya Salad or any meat or fish dish.

Rice with Peas and Omelette Strips

KAO PAT MAE KLANG

PREPARATION TIME: 40 MINUTES
SERVES 4

350 g/12 oz/1½ cups long-grain rice

225 g/8 oz/½ lb button mushrooms

75 ml/5 tbsp oil

225 g/8 oz/2 cups peas (shelled fresh or frozen)

4 eggs, beaten

30 ml/2 tbsp soy sauce

30 ml/2 tbsp fish sauce (see page 24)

30 ml/2 tbsp tamarind juice (see page 23)

Salt

1 Boil the rice in plenty of salted water for about 15 minutes until tender. Drain, rinse with boiling water and drain again.

2 Meanwhile, fry (sauté) the mushrooms in 45 ml/3 tbsp of the oil in a frying pan (skillet) until juices have evaporated. Add the peas and stir fry for 1–2 minutes.

3 Heat remaining oil in a separate frying pan (skillet) and fry the beaten eggs until set. Remove from the pan and cut into thin strips.

4 Mix the rice with the mushrooms and the peas and season with soy and fish sauce as well as the tamarind juice. Season with salt if necessary.

5 Put the rice into a bowl and garnish with the omelette strips.

Fried Rice with Crab

KAO PHAT PU

PREPARATION TIME: 20 MINUTES
PLUS COOKING TIME FOR RICE
SERVES 4

60 ml/4 tbsp oil

400 g/14 oz/3½ cups cold
boiled rice (200 g/7 oz/scant
1 cup uncooked weight)

300 g/11 oz/scant 1½ cups crab
meat (canned or from two
cooked crabs, see recipe
page 113)

3 eggs, beaten

Salt

2 spring onions (scallions),
sliced

30 ml/2 tbsp fish sauce (see
page 24)

5–10 ml/1–2 tsp sugar

grated rind of 1 lime or small
lemon

SAUCE:

2–4 dried chillies, crushed

60 ml/4 tbsp fish sauce

15 ml/1 tbsp lime or lemon
juice

¼ cucumber, halved and sliced

A few coriander (cilantro)
leaves to garnish

1 Heat the oil in a large frying pan (skillet), add the rice and the crab meat and stir-fry for 4 minutes.

2 Push rice and crab to one side and pour beaten eggs into the pan. Stir and allow the eggs to set, then mix with the rice and the crab and season lightly.

3 Add the spring onions, the fish sauce, the sugar and the lime rind.

4 Mix the sauce ingredients together.

5 Spoon the fried rice onto a serving plate. Arrange the cucumber slices around. Pour the sauce over the rice and sprinkle with a few coriander leaves.

Fried Rice with Seafood

KAO PAD LAE AHARNT TA LAY

PREPARATION TIME: 30 MINUTES
PLUS COOKING TIME FOR RICE
SERVES 4

---

60 ml/4 tbsp oil

1 onion, chopped

3 garlic cloves, crushed

600 g/1¼ lb seafood cocktail
(thawed if frozen)

5 ml/1 tsp grated galgant root
or 2.5 ml/½ tsp ground
ginger

5 ml/1 tsp finely chopped
lemon grass

2.5 ml/½ tsp white pepper

2.5 ml/½ tsp cayenne

30–45 ml/2–3 tbsp tomato
ketchup (catsup)

30 ml/2 tbsp fish sauce (see
page 24)

600 g/1¼ lb cold boiled rice
(300 g/11 oz/1⅓ cups
uncooked weight)

2–3 spring onions (scallions),
chopped

A few coriander leaves to
garnish

1 Heat the oil in a frying pan (skillet) and fry (sauté) the onion until golden. Add the garlic.

2 Add the seafood cocktail and stir-fry for 2 minutes. Season with galgant root, lemon grass, pepper and cayenne and fry until all the liquid has evaporated.

3 Add the ketchup and the fish sauce and cook, stirring for 2 minutes.

4 Add the rice and mix well. Cook gently for 3 minutes, stirring until the rice is hot. Add a little water if too dry.

5 Scatter the chopped spring onion over and garnish with a few coriander leaves before serving.

Rice Noodles with Coconut Milk

MI KRATI

PREPARATION TIME: 35 MINUTES
SERVES 4

200 g/7 oz/1¾ cups rice noodles

500 ml/17 fl oz/2¼ cups coconut milk (see page 18)

50 g/2 oz/½ cup creamed coconut

4 shallots or 1-2 onions, finely chopped

300 g/11 oz/scant ¾ lb lean pork or chicken, cut in thin strips

300 g/11 oz/scant ¾ lb pak soi or Swiss chard stalks, chopped

150 g/5 oz/⅔ cup tofu (soya bean curd), diced

300 g/11 oz/2¾ cups soya bean sprouts (fresh or drained canned)

Salt

15 ml/1 tbsp sugar

30-45 ml/2-3 tbsp tamarind juice (see page 23)

3-6 dried chillies, crushed

150 g/5 oz/scant 1 cup salted soya beans (from Asian food shops)

4 eggs, beaten

30 ml/2 tbsp oil

a few horapa or basil leaves and lemon wedges to garnish

1 Pour boiling water over the rice noodles and leave to stand for 4 minutes then drain.

2 Warm the coconut milk in a saucepan, add the creamed coconut and leave to melt.

3 Add the shallots, meat, tofu and stalks, bring to the boil, reduce heat and simmer for 10 to 15 minutes.

4 Add the salt and sugar, tamarind juice, chillies, salted beans and soya bean sprouts and stir well. Place half the sauce on one side.

5 Fry (sauté) the eggs in the oil in a frying pan (skillet) to make a thin omelette. Remove from the frying pan and cut into thin strips.

6 Mix the rice noodles with the one half of the sauce and cook and stir for 1 to 2 minutes. Pour into a bowl and pour the other half of the sauce over it.

7 Garnish with the omelette strips, horapa leaves and lemon wedges.

Rice Noodles with Broccoli

KUI TIAO RAD NAR

PREPARATION TIME: 40 MINUTES
SERVES 4

---

150 g/5 oz/1¼ cups rice noodles

1 small onion, finely chopped

3 garlic cloves, crushed

75 ml/5 tbsp oil

450 g/1 lb chicken breast or pork fillet, cut in thin strips

Salt

100 ml/3½ fl oz/6½ tbsp water

300 g/11 oz/scant ¾ lb broccoli cut in small florets

45 ml/3 tbsp fish sauce (see page 24)

45 ml/3 tbsp soy sauce

15 ml/1 tbsp sugar

2.5 ml/½ tsp white pepper

2 fresh red chillies, seeded and sliced into thin rings

1 Pour boiling water over the rice noodles and leave to soak for 3–4 minutes. Drain and cut into fairly small pieces.

2 Heat 45 ml/3 tbsp of the oil in a frying pan (skillet), and fry (sauté) the onion until golden. Add the garlic and noodles and stir-fry for 10 minutes. Separate the noodles using two forks.

3 Fry (sauté) the meat quickly to brown in a second frying pan in the remaining oil. Season with salt and stir in the water. Add to the noodles.

4 Cook the broccoli in boiling salted water until just tender. Drain and add to the meat and noodles. Turn up the heat and add the fish and soy sauces, the sugar and pepper. Stir well.

5 Sprinkle the chillies over the dish just before serving.

Rice Noodles with Minced Meat Sauce

KUI TIAO NEUG SAB

PREPARATION TIME: 50 MINUTES
SERVES 4

450 g/1 lb/4 cups minced (ground) beef

75 ml/5 tbsp soy sauce

5 ml/1 tsp curry powder or garam masala

5 ml/1 tsp salt

5 ml/1 tsp black pepper

30–45 ml/2–3 tbsp tapioca or plain (all-purpose) flour

75 ml/5 tbsp oil

50 g/2 oz/½ cup sliced celery

4 garlic cloves, crushed

300 ml/½ pt/1¼ cups beef or chicken stock

15 ml/1 tbsp sugar

A few coriander (cilantro) leaves, chopped

450 g/1 lb/4 cups wide rice noodles

30 ml/2 tbsp soy sauce

4 small dried chillies, crushed

30 ml/2 tbsp red wine vinegar

1 Mix the minced meat with the soy sauce, curry, salt, pepper and the flour and leave to stand for a few minutes.

2 Heat 45 ml/3 tbsp of the oil in a frying pan (skillet) and brown the meat in it stirring continually.

3 Add the celery and the garlic together with the stock to the meat. Sprinkle with sugar and simmer for 15 minutes.

4 Meanwhile pour boiling water over the noodles and leave to soak for 10–20 minutes. Drain.

5 Heat remaining 30 ml/2 tbsp of the oil in a frying pan (skillet), add the soy sauce and turn the noodles in it until they are soft, about 5 minutes.

6 Place the noodles in a bowl, pour over the sauce and sprinkle with the coriander.

7 Mix the chillies with the vinegar and pour over before serving.

Fried Rice Noodles with Pork and Prawns

KUI TIAO PAD MOO KAB PU

PREPARATION TIME: 1 HOUR
SERVES 4

90 ml/6 tbsp oil

1 onion, finely chopped

225 g/8 oz/2 cups finely diced lean pork

4 garlic cloves, crushed

150 g/5 oz/1¼ cups peeled prawns (shrimp), chopped

50 g/2 oz/½ cup soya bean sprouts (fresh or drained, canned)

100 g/4 oz/1 cup shredded Chinese leaves (stem lettuce)

3–4 dried chillies, crushed

15 ml/1 tbsp salted beans (from Asian and other specialist food shops)

15 ml/1 tbsp vinegar

15 ml/1 tbsp fish sauce (see page 24)

15 ml/1 tbsp palm or soft brown sugar

15 ml/1 tbsp lemon juice

Salt

100 g/4 oz/½ cup tofu (soya bean curd), cut in strips

150 g/5 oz/1¼ cups rice noodles

A few coriander (cilantro) leaves to garnish

1 Heat 15 ml/1 tbsp of the oil in a large frying pan (skillet) and fry (sauté) the onion until golden. Add the meat and the garlic and stir-fry for 1 minute.

2 Add the prawns, soya bean sprouts, Chinese leaves and chillies and fry for a further 2–3 minutes.

3 Add the salted beans, vinegar, fish sauce, sugar and lemon juice. Season to taste with salt and keep warm.

4 Fry (sauté) the tofu in 30 ml/2 tbsp of the remaining oil until crispy brown and place on one side.

5 Heat the remaining oil in a separate pan and fry the dry rice noodles stirring continually for 3–4 minutes. Add sufficient water until they become soft (about 100 ml/3½ fl oz/6½ tbsp), and stir for a further 2 minutes until cooked.

6 Add the meat and prawn mixture to the noodles, stir well and place over the fried tofu strips. Sprinkle with coriander leaves to garnish.

Fried Rice Noodles in Thai Style

KUI TIAO THAI

PREPARATION TIME: 45 MINUTES
SERVES 4

1 onion, finely chopped

4 garlic cloves, crushed

90 ml/6 tbsp oil

300 g/11 oz/2¾ cups rice noodles

120 ml/4 fl oz/½ cup water

400 g/14 oz/scant 1 lb pork fillet or shoulder

100 g/4 oz/¼ lb white radish or turnip

225 g/8 oz/½ lb courgettes (zucchini)

50 g/2 oz/½ cup chopped celery

100 g/4 oz/½ cup tofu (soya bean curd), diced

175 g/6 oz/1½ cups soya bean sprouts

Salt

3 duck or size 1 hen eggs, beaten

60 ml/4 tbsp vinegar

15 ml/1 tbsp sugar

60 ml/4 tbsp fish sauce (see page 24)

40 g/1½ oz/⅓ cup unsalted peanuts

4 red fresh chillies , seeded and cut into thin rings

1 Fry (sauté) the onion and garlic until lightly golden in 30 ml/2 tbsp of the oil. Add the dry noodles, press with fish slice or wok stirrer and stir-fry for 5 minutes. Then add the water and cook the noodles for 10 minutes.

2 Cut the pork into thin strips and cut the radish and the courgettes into thin slices.

3 Heat the remaining oil in a separate pan and fry the meat quickly to brown. Add the radish, soya bean sprouts, celery, tofu and courgettes and stir-fry for 5 minutes. Season with salt and remove from the heat.

4 Heat the remaining oil in a separate pan. Pour in the eggs, stir until thoroughly set.

5 Place the frying pan with the meat once more onto the heat, add the noodles, and the scrambled eggs and mix well. Season with vinegar, sugar and fish sauce.

6 Grind the peanuts coarsely in a coffee grinder (or chop with an electric chopper). Sprinkle over the dish with the chillies.

Rice Noodles with King Prawns

KUI TIAO PAD KUNG

PREPARATION TIME: 35 MINUTES
SERVES 4

150 g/5 oz/1¼ cups rice noodles

16 king prawns (jumbo shrimp) with shells

60 ml/4 tbsp oil

2 shallots or 1 small onion, finely chopped

4 garlic cloves, crushed

60 ml/4 tbsp chilli sauce (ready made)

60 ml/4 tbsp tomato ketchup (catsup)

60 ml/4 tbsp fish sauce (see page 24)

15 ml/1 tbsp palm or soft brown sugar

Pinch of cayenne

Salt

250 g/9 oz/2¼ cups soya bean sprouts

45 ml/3 tbsp chopped (snipped) chives

1 Pour boiling water over the rice noodles and leave to soak for 3–4 minutes. Drain.

2 Shell the king prawns, leaving on the tail fins and remove the black vein down each back.

3 Heat the oil in a frying pan (skillet) and stir-fry the noodles in it until golden brown, then remove with a draining spoon and place on one side.

4 Fry (sauté) the shallots in the same pan until golden. Add the garlic, fry for 1 minute, then add the chilli sauce, ketchup and fish sauce. Season with the sugar, cayenne and salt if necessary.

5 Add the king prawns to the frying pan and heat for 2–3 minutes then stir. Should the sauce be too thick, add a little water.

6 Return the noodles to the frying pan and mix well.

7 Arrange everything on a serving plate and garnish with soya bean sprouts. Sprinkle with the chives before serving.

Rice Noodles with Crab

KUI TIAO

PREPARATION TIME: 45 MINUTES
SERVES 4

SPICE PASTE:

5 dried chillies, crushed

5 shallots or 1–2 onions, finely chopped

5 garlic cloves, crushed

2.5 ml/½ tsp salt

400 g/14 oz/3½ cups rice noodles

300 g/11 oz/2¾ cups soya bean sprouts (fresh or drained, canned)

200 g/7 oz/1¾ cups shredded Chinese leaves (stem lettuce)

600 g/1¼ lb/crab meat (from about 3 fresh crabs or canned)

90 ml/6 tbsp oil

75 ml/5 tbsp tamarind juice (see page 23)

75 ml/5 tbsp fish sauce (see page 24)

30 ml/2 tbsp palm or soft brown sugar

3 lemons, cut in wedges

1 Pound the chillies, shallots and garlic with the salt in a pestle and mortar or in a bowl with the end of a rolling pin.

2 Pour boiling water over the noodles and leave to soak for 3–4 minutes. Drain.

3 Heat 45 ml/3 tbsp of the oil in a frying pan (skillet) and fry (sauté) the spice paste. Add the crab meat and stir-fry for 1 minute.

4 Heat the remaining 45 ml/3 tbsp of oil in a second frying pan (skillet) and fry (sauté) the dry noodles. Add the soya bean sprouts and the Chinese leaves and stir-fry for 3 minutes.

5 Add the crab mixture to the noodles, and season with the tamarind juice, fish sauce and sugar and stir-fry for 1–2 minutes until hot.

6 Spoon the noodles with the crab meat into bowls and garnish with lemon wedges.

Rice Noodles with Fish Sauce

KHANOM JEEN NAM YA

PREPARATION TIME: 1 HOUR
PLUS SOAKING TIME
SERVES 4

100 g/4 oz/¼ lb dried salt cod

Oil for frying

7 shallots or 2–3 onions, finely chopped

10–15 garlic cloves, crushed

5–10 dried small chillies, crushed

2 cm/¾ in piece fresh galgant root, grated or 2.5 ml/½ tsp ground ginger

25 g/1 oz/2 tbsp lemon grass, finely chopped

30 ml/2 tbsp chopped mint

5 ml/1 tsp salt

15 ml/1 tbsp prawn (shrimp) paste (see page 25)

120 ml/4 fl oz/½ cup water

400 g/14 oz/3½ cups fresh grated or desiccated (shredded) coconut

200 g/7 oz/scant ½ lb white fish fillet

400 g/14 oz/3½ cups rice noodles

100 g/4 oz/1 cup cut green beans

100 g/4 oz/1 cup shredded savoy cabbage

100 g/4 oz/1 cup soya bean sprouts (fresh or drained canned)

¼ cucumber, sliced

1 green (bell) pepper, seeded and diced

2 hard-boiled (hard-cooked) eggs, sliced

A few horapa or basil leaves and fresh red chillies (optional)

1 Soak the dried fish for 2–3 hours in water, then drain, dab dry, pull into fine threads and fry them in a little of the oil.

2 Add the shallots, garlic, chillies, galgant root, lemon grass, mint, salt and prawn paste and the water and cook gently, stirring occasionally for 20 minutes until soft. Purée in a blender or food processor then sieve (strain) to remove any bits.

3 Scald the coconut flesh with a good 500 ml/17 fl oz/2¼ cups boiling water. Pass through a sieve (strainer) lined with muslin (cheesecloth) and squeeze out the coconut juice with the help of the cloth.

4 Poach the fish fillet in a little salted water until cooked. Mix the fish with the dried fish purée. Add the coconut milk and fish cooking water and bring to the boil. Stirring all the time in an open saucepan reduce until it thickens.

5 Place the rice noodles in boiling water. Leave to swell for 3–4 minutes and then drain. Cook the beans in boiling salted water until just tender, about 5 minutes, drain. Cook the cabbage in boiling water until just cooked, about 8 minutes, drain.

6 Arrange the noodles, vegetables, eggs and horapa leaves on a large serving plate and place the fish sauce in a small dish alongside. Everyone takes some of the noodles on a plate, pours the sauce on top and arranges the eggs and vegetables around. Add a sprinkling of red chillies if liked.

COOK'S TIP: Use canned coconut milk instead of making your own if you prefer.

Sweets and Drinks

At the end of a traditional celebration
Thai meal a variety of sweets are served –
at least one of which will
consist of fresh fruit.
The refreshing juices, for which you will
find recipes in this chapter, are drunk
from very early until late: before, during
and after meals.

Bananas in Coconut Milk

KLUAI BUAT CHEE

PREPARATION TIME: 15 MINUTES
PLUS CHILLING TIME
SERVES 4

4 ripe bananas

30 ml/2 tbsp sugar

Pinch of salt

250 ml/8 fl oz/1 cup coconut milk (see page 18)

1–2 drops jasmine essence (extract) or rose water

30 ml/2 tbsp sesame seeds

1 Peel the bananas and cut them into slices about 1 cm/½ in thick. Place in a saucepan and sprinkle with sugar and salt.

2 Add the coconut milk and the jasmine essence and cook for 2–3 minutes.

3 Leave to cool then chill for about 1 hour.

4 Dry-fry the sesame seeds in a frying pan (skillet) until golden brown and sprinkle over the bananas.

Fried Bananas

KLUAI TORD

PREPARATION TIME: 15 MINUTES
SERVES 4-6

4 bananas not too ripe

30 ml/2 tbsp butter

15 ml/1 tbsp palm or soft
brown sugar

juice of 2 limes or 1 lemon

45-60 ml/3-4 tbsp fresh, grated
or desiccated (shredded)
coconut

1 Peel the bananas and halve lengthways.

2 Heat the butter in a frying pan (skillet) and fry the bananas on both sides for 3 minutes, until they are light brown and transparent.

3 Add the sugar and the lime juice and stir until the sugar has dissolved.

4 Arrange the bananas on plates, pour the sauce over and sprinkle with coconut.

Pumpkin Pudding

KANON FAGTHONG

PREPARATION TIME: 1¾ HOURS
SERVES 4

400 g/14 oz/3½ cups pumpkin, seeded and diced

200 g/7 oz/1¾ cups desiccated (shredded) coconut

400 ml/14 fl oz/1¾ cups boiling water

150 g/5 oz/1¼ cups flour (if possible half and half tapioca and plain (all-purpose) flour)

2.5 ml/½ tsp salt

100 g/4 oz/½ cup sugar

Oil for greasing

1 Steam or boil the pumpkin for about 25 minutes until it is very soft.

2 Scald the coconut with the boiling water, leave for a short time and then strain in a sieve (strainer) lined with muslin (cheesecloth). Press out well, collect the coconut milk and reserve 50 g/2 oz/½ cup of the pressed out coconut shreds.

3 Purée the pumpkin with the coconut milk in a blender or food processor, then stir in the flour, salt and sugar.

4 Grease lightly a shallow, heat resistant dish, fill with the pumpkin mixture and sprinkle the reserved coconut over the top. Cover the dish firmly with foil. Bake at 200°C/400°F/gas mark 6 for about 1 hour and serve warm.

Rice Boats with Bananas

KAO TOM MAT

PREPARATION TIME: 1 HOUR
PLUS SOAKING TIME
SERVES 6-8

450 g/1 lb pudding rice

400 g/14 oz/3½ cups
desiccated (shredded) coconut

1 litre/1¾ pts/4¼ cups water

2.5 ml/½ tsp salt

150 g/5 oz/⅔ cup sugar

300 ml/½ pt/1¼ cups milk

3-4 bananas

oil for brushing

100 g/4 oz/1 cup canned,
    drained black boiled beans

*COOK'S TIPS: In Thailand banana
leaves are used in the place of foil.
Here in the autumn, washed sweetcorn
(corn) cob leaves can be used. These
must be tied well with kitchen thread.*

*The use of beans in a dessert may
appear strange to some. Use raisins
instead if you prefer.*

1 Wash the pudding rice and leave for 1-2 hours in cold water to swell. Drain.

2 Scald the coconut with the boiling water, leave for 5 minutes and then pass through a sieve (strainer) lined with muslin (cheesecloth) into a bowl.

3 Mix the coconut milk with salt, sugar and milk in a saucepan. Add the drained rice and simmer, stirring until the mixture has absorbed all the liquid (about 20 minutes).

4 Peel the bananas, cut first diagonally, then along the length, so that each banana is divided into four pieces.

5 Cut squares of foil about 13 cm/ 5 in and lightly brush with oil.

6 Place 30-45 ml/2-3 tbsp of the rice mixture on each of the foil squares, place a piece of banana on it and then cover it with a little more rice. Press a few black beans into the rice. Roll up the foil, fold in the sides and close tightly.

7 Place the little packets in a steamer and steam the rice for 30 minutes or place them in a greased heat resistant dish, cover and place in a water bath in the oven at 230°C/450°F/gas mark 8 for about the same length of time.

Rice with Mangoes

MAMUANG KAO NIEO

PREPARATION TIME: 1 HOUR
PLUS SOAKING AND CHILLING TIME
SERVES 4–6

300 g/11 oz/1⅓ cups pudding rice

300 ml/½ pt/1¼ cups coconut milk (see page 18)

100 g/4 oz/½ cup sugar

Pinch of salt

4 ripe mangoes, peeled and cut in segments round the stones (pits)

60–75 ml/4–5 tbsp desiccated (shredded) coconut

1 Wash the pudding rice and leave to soak for 1–2 hours in cold water. Drain and cook in one and a half times its volume of water for about 20 minutes stirring. Drain if necessary.

2 Reduce the coconut milk by boiling down to about one third of the amount, then add sugar and salt and stir to dissolve. Mix the pudding rice with the coconut milk and leave to stand for 30 minutes.

3 Arrange the rice on a plate, place the mango segments on top and sprinkle everything with coconut flakes. Chill for 1–2 hours before serving.

Fruit Salad

SALAD POLAMAI

PREPARATION TIME: 40 MINUTES
PLUS CHILLING TIME
SERVES 4-6

2 ripe mangoes

1 small pineapple

3 large oranges

1 small honeydew melon

2 apples

2 bananas

Juice of 3 limes or small
lemons

A few lemon balm or mint
leaves

1 Peel the mangos, remove the fruit flesh from the stones (pits) and cut diagonally into segments. Cut off the top and bottom of the pineapple and using a sharp knife cut away the peel generously. Cut the fruit into quarters, cut out core and cut the pineapple into chunks.

2 Peel the oranges like apples completely removing the white pith. Cut the fruit along the dividing skin and ease out the segments, catching the juice.

3 Halve the melon, scrape out the seeds (pits), remove the fruit from the peel and cut into pieces. Peel the apples and quarter. Remove the cores and dice the apple quarters. Peel the bananas and cut into slices.

4 Mix all the fruit very carefully together. Pour the lime juice and the collected orange juice over the mixed salad and chill for 1 hour.

5 Just before serving, toss lightly and decorate with lemon balm or mint leaves.

Coconut Macaroons

KHANOM SAMANAT

PREPARATION TIME: 35 MINUTES
SERVES 6-8

300 g/11 oz/2¾ cups desiccated (shredded) coconut

4 egg whites

150 g/5 oz/⅔ cup caster (superfine) sugar

15-30 ml/1-2 tbsp cocoa (unsweetened chocolate) powder

15 ml/1 tbsp lemon juice

1 Preheat the oven to 160°C/ 325°F/gas mark 3.

2 Dry-fry the coconut in a frying pan (skillet) until golden brown and leave to cool a little. Beat the egg whites to a stiff foam.

3 Carefully fold all the ingredients into the egg white, so that they are well mixed.

4 Using a small spoon cut out mounds and place on a greased baking sheet. Bake until golden brown – about 30 minutes.

Oranges in Jasmin Syrup

NAM CHUAM DOK MALEE

PREPARATION TIME: 40 MINUTES
SERVES 4

4 oranges

150 g/5 oz/⅔ cup granulated sugar

100 ml/3½ fl oz/6½ tbsp water

2–3 drops jasmine essence (extract) or rose water

A few rose or lemon balm leaves

A few ice cubes

COOK'S TIP: *Instead of the oranges three ripe mangoes can be used. They are peeled and the flesh cut into segments and arranged like the oranges.*

1 Peel the oranges like apples, removing the white pith and cut the fruit either diagonally in slices or remove the segments.

2 Bring the sugar to boil in the water and simmer until a thick liquid syrup has formed (up to 30 minutes over a gentle heat). Then leave to cool and perfume with jasmine essence or rose water.

3 Place the ice cubes in a plastic bag and crush fine with a hammer or a rolling pin.

4 Arrange the orange pieces on shallow dishes, pour over the syrup and sprinkle the crushed ice on top. Garnish with jasmine flowers or with rose leaves, lemon balm or mint leaves. Serve straight away.

Lychees in Cream

LEENCHEE LOI MEK

PREPARATION TIME: 30 MINUTES
PLUS CHILLING TIME
SERVES 4

5 eggs, separated

90 ml/6 tbsp sugar

450 ml/¾ pt/2 cups
  unsweetened evaporated
  milk

20 fresh, peeled or drained
  canned lychees

1 Whisk the egg whites with 15 ml/1 tbsp sugar to a stiff foam and place in a sieve (strainer). Place over a pan of gently simmering water, cover with a lid and steam the meringue until it is firm (this takes about 5–10 minutes). Then place it on one side.

2 Whisk the egg yolks with the rest of the sugar and the evaporated milk over a pan of hot water to a smooth thick cream.

3 Place the lychees in a flat dish and cover in the egg yolk cream.

4 Divide the egg white foam on top and chill for 1 hour.

Mangoes with Sweet Fish Sauce

MA MAMUANG NAM PLA WAN

PREPARATION TIME: 30 MINUTES
PLUS CHILLING TIME
SERVES 4

100 ml/3½ fl oz/6½ tbsp fish sauce (see page 24)

100 ml/3½ fl oz/6½ tbsp water

50–75 g/2–3 oz/¼–⅓ cup sugar

1 shallot, finely chopped

30 ml/2 tbsp prawn (shrimp) paste (see page 25)

2 dried chillies, crushed

2 ripe mangoes, peeled and sliced

1 Mix the fish sauce with the water and the sugar and bring to the boil.

2 Add the shallot and simmer gently for about 15–20 minutes until a thick syrup is obtained.

3 Mix in the prawn paste and the crushed chillies. Chill.

4 Place the mango segments in a dish and add the sauce.

Gooseberry Juice

NAM MAYOM

PREPARATION TIME: 30 MINUTES
PLUS CHILLING TIME
SERVES 4

300 g/11 oz/scant 1½ cups
gooseberries, topped and
tailed

750 ml/1¼ pts/3 cups water

250 g/9 oz/good 1 cup sugar

2.5 ml/½ tsp salt

To serve: ice cubes

1 Bring the gooseberries to the boil in the water. Leave to cook for 20 minutes.

2 Purée everything in a blender or food processor (or in the saucepan with a hand mixer). Place in a sieve (strainer) and drain the juice. Press out the gooseberries well.

3 Add sugar and salt to the juice, bring this once more to the boil and leave to simmer very gently for 10 minutes. Leave to cool, chill for at least 2 hours and serve with ice cubes.

Coconut Ice

A I S A K R I M G A T I

PREPARATION TIME: 30–40 MINUTES
PLUS FREEZING TIME
SERVES 4

---

1 coconut (about 750 g/1½ lb)

3 eggs, separated

75 g/3 oz/⅓ cup sugar

100 ml/3½ fl oz/6½ tbsp milk

To serve: tamarind syrup
    (obtainable in Asian shops)

1 Open the coconut, drain the coconut milk and use elsewhere. Carefully remove the white fruit flesh from the brown shell, rinse briefly and place in cold water.

2 Bet the egg yolks together with the sugar with a hand mixer until thick and pale.

3 Purée the coconut pieces in portions in a blender or food processor and add to the egg yolk mixture. Add the milk and stir.

4 Whisk the egg whites to a stiff foam and fold into the yolk mixture. Freeze in a suitable container for 3–4 hours.

5 Leave the ice to defrost for about 20 minutes before serving, then pour tamarind syrup on top and serve.

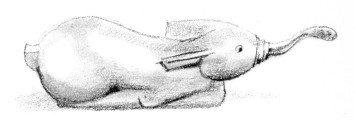

Index